The Complete Entlebucher Mountain Dog Book

(Entlebucher Sennenhund)

A guide to understanding your dog

Rosemary J. Kind

Printed in the United Kingdom

First Printing, 2017 Alfie Dog Limited

The author can be found at: www.rjkind.co.uk

Cover image: Front – Victory Megan vom Kornried. Back – Baika-Susi vom Arvenstock, Wilma vom Rickental, Valeria vom Rickental

ISBN 978-1-909894-37-2

Published by
Alfie Dog Limited
Schilde Lodge,
Tholthorpe,
North Yorkshire,
YO61 1SN
UNITED KINGDOM

Tel: +44 (0) 207 193 33 90

DEDICATION

To
Sonja van den Durpel

Thank you for trusting us with our precious Alfie.

and

To
Maja Kleinjenni

Words are simply not enough to express my gratitude for all you have taught me about this wonderful breed.

CONTENTS

Gina Graber with Susi and Käthi (Photo Gina Graber)

In Switzerland each year there are a number of Festival Parades where the Entlebuchers take part, with owners wearing traditional Swiss dress from their home region. Here Gina is wearing the 'Sunday best' from Aargau.

ACKNOWLEDGMENTS

There are very many people to whom I am indebted. It would not be possible to name them all. However, Maja Kleinjenni, Sonja van den Durpel and Herma Cornelese have taught me so much about this beautiful breed and I could not have achieved any of this without them.

I am grateful to so many members of the Swiss Club (Schweizerischer Klub für Entlebucher Sennenhunde) who have helped both with our work in developing the breed in the UK and with this book.

My thanks to Claude Schelling of the Klinik für Reproduktionsmedizin in Zurich, for his introduction to their work on breed health.

None of this would have happened without Mike Caughlin, Kristina Fields, Chris Platt, Adrianne Klijn and Sue Kendal – thank you for your work in setting up the UK Club.

For the information on the breed in other countries I would like to thank Max Heller - Switzerland, Herma Cornelese - The Netherlands, Ute Rüegg - Sweden, Tatyana Nepakhareva - Russia, Bohdana Stoklasová and Pavel Pečenkovi - Czech Republic, Lisbet Aarum - Norway, Céline Heulin – France.

Robyn Burnett and Sarah Fulker thank you for being as passionate about these dogs as I am and doing so much in the UK for the breed.

Avril Batty-Hardy thank you for all your help with Shadow's litters and convincing me I could do it when I started to panic.

My writing buddies Patsy, Lynne, Suzy and Sheila as always I am grateful for your unstinting support.

Alfie, Shadow, Megan, Aristotle and Wilma thank you for the training you have given me.

Also, thank you to Serge Renggli for making so many photos available to me. David Gibbins for coming to take the author photo at Entlebuch Station. The many other people who have kindly allowed me to use their photos are credited on the photos concerned – thank you all.

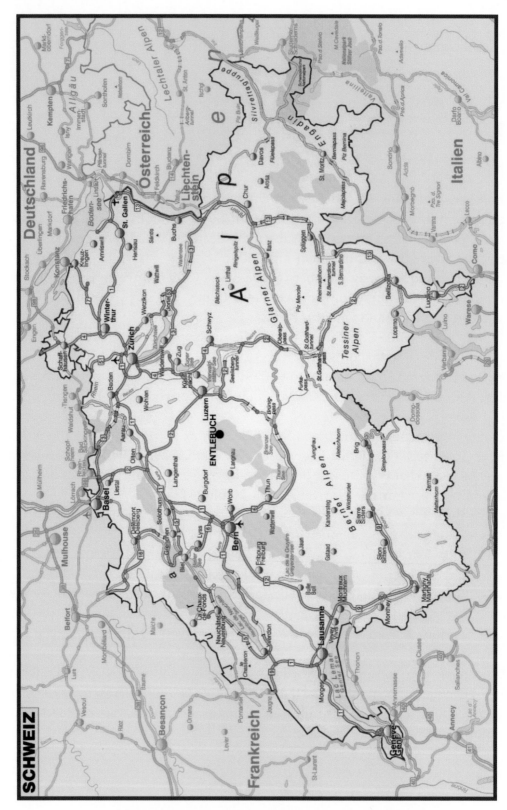

Map of Switzerland showing the location of Entlebuch

INTRODUCTION

This book could have had other titles such as 'A guide to understanding your dog' or 'What it's like to live with this special breed'. It also contains a fair amount of dog psychology gleaned from observation and having had some of the best four-legged teachers in the world. It could equally be entitled 'The Trials and Tribulations of Developing a Dog Breed in the UK.'! I've written the book in an attempt to share my love of this wonderful breed and to help others to get the best out of their relationships with their dogs. I also hope it might help in some small way toward the ongoing work of ensuring a strong and healthy future for what is in relative terms a very small gene pool.

I have been asked why I would want a pedigree dog in the first place. Basically, with a breed you have a good idea what general temperament you will get and the particular qualities. With a non-pedigree you don't - even if you know the parents, it could take after one rather than the other or have a grandparent you really weren't expecting. After that, I know I love the intelligence of the working breeds and their approach to life. We are most in tune with each other. I also needed a dog that would be as devoted to me as I am to him. One that is great with children

Torfheide Duchess

and only guards when that is actually really needed. I needed a dog who was low on allergy problems, keeps himself clean and needs next to no grooming, a dog who doesn't suffer from any skin conditions, so doesn't really smell. I wanted a dog who will never leave my side, is deeply affectionate and loves being cuddled; one who enjoys walking but is just as happy to relax, who isn't yappy or whiney and as a bonus is incredibly good looking…

My love affair with the breed began in about 1999 when I read 'The MacDonald

Encyclopaedia of Dogs'. I read the description, saw the picture and firmly believed I'd found my perfect dog. Nearly twenty years later, and with a house full of Entlebuchers, I'm quite convinced it was one of the soundest decisions I've ever made. Of course, Entlebuchers aren't for everyone. They are lively, intelligent and very strong, as well as being at times strong-willed. However, I've always liked to be kept on my toes and having a dog that's brighter than I am is a very good way to do that.

Although this book is a factual reference book on the breed, it is also dotted with anecdotes and stories which reveal the wonders of sharing your life with these amazing dogs. You can read under 'My Story' why I came to be so determined to develop the breed in the UK, but needless to say without those events I would not have come to write this book. Whether you have bought the book to dip into or to read from cover to cover, I sincerely hope that you will enjoy it. I welcome any communication about the breed, so feel free to get in touch.

Rosemary Kind September 2017
rosjkind@gmail.com

Throughout the book I will refer to the dogs as 'he' rather than 'she' or 'it'. Please take 'he' to embrace both male and female. I'm sorry, but I cannot bear to describe my dogs as 'it'!

Binto Sämi v Grundstiegeli - father of Shadow's 'B' litter (Photo Serge Renggli)

PRONUNCIATION

Of course, if you are Swiss and from the German speaking part of the country you may wonder why the rest of us pronounce the name of the breed incorrectly. On many occasions, friends have tried to perfect my pronunciation, but alas to no avail. I'm only grateful I come somewhere close. Entlebucher is roughly pronounced ENT-leh-boo-cur. To my ear the 'leh' sound is roughly as I would say the word 'lay', 'boo' is not as in England we would say when trying to surprise someone, but more an 'ou' sound and the 'cur' is not a hard 'c'. The final syllable is an especially unusual pronunciation for an English speaker. The 'c' is a softer sound as Scots tell us is in the word Loch. It is not 'lock'. How 'bucher' is not pronounced, that I hear regularly, is any of 'busher', 'butcher' or 'boosher' or even 'booka'.

Sadly, due to the difficulty of the pronunciation for an English speaking person, the full name 'Entlebucher' is sometimes abbreviated, but to me that is a great shame.

My story

When I came across the breed through 'The Encyclopaedia of Dogs' in 1999, my research turned up that there were none in the UK at that time and, to be honest, I was not in a position to look after one anyway. However, the more I read, the more I became convinced this was the breed for me. I did start to wonder whether there was a possibility of my going to live and work somewhere else in Europe so I could have one, but I could not think of a way to make it work. All that changed in 2005 when my husband had the opportunity to work in Belgium. Other than saying I needed to have trees where we lived, I made only one condition, I would have an Entlebucher Mountain Dog. The timing was perfect as I was also making the change to work for myself from home and would therefore be around all the time to be with my dog. I got in touch with the Entlebucher Club in Belgium to join the waiting list. Within a few months of moving, Einstein Van de Tiendenschuur, known as Alfie, came into our lives. He was everything I had dreamed of and nearly twelve years later he still is. From day one, he and I were inseparable. He was always quite a serious puppy and from that first day we used that to good

effect by starting to write his daily diary as an internet blog.

Alfie's Diary (www.alfiedog.me.uk) was originally intended to keep our friends and family informed about life in Belgium and as a discipline for me to make sure that, as an author, I wrote every day. Over the years it has become much more than that and it has never been hard to try to represent the world through Alfie's eyes. It was recently announced to be number three in the UK's top ten Pet Blogs.

(Photo Red Jester Photography)

By the time we moved back to the UK in January 2008 I was so addicted to the breed, that I could not bear the thought that I would never be able to have another if anything happened to Alfie. No one was breeding them in the UK at the time, although there had, as you will read, been one litter. When I was asked if I would like to take on a three year old girl who had been imported for breeding, I jumped at the chance. I knew nothing about dog

4

breeding in those days, but that wasn't going to hold me back. However, what I wasn't aware of was that Marbella was an escape artist and of a very nervous disposition. Unfortunately, at the first opportunity Marbella bolted and ran. To begin with Alfie ran after her, but she was a dog on a mission and she wasn't going to stop. Alfie came back alone and I spent the next few days and nights searching for her. It is a very sad story, as on the fourth day we heard from the railway engineers in York that she had been found at the side of the track. When it happened we barely knew her, but for me it opened the floodgates to a grieving process. A few months earlier my husband and I had come to the end of our own fertility treatment and concluded that I would never be able to have children of my own. In many ways, I was seeing dog breeding as a substitute. Losing Marbella hit me very hard, but it had a very positive outcome. I'm not a negative person by nature and out of the adversity came the determination that I would do whatever I could to help to develop the Entlebucher breed and that I would let nothing stand in my way. I was on a mission. I didn't have a breeding dog. I didn't know anything about dog breeding. I knew very few people in the breed. There was no UK Club.

Aisha Princess of Beauty (Shadow) (Photo Sabine Mancosu)

Thankfully over the years, whilst there have been a fair few setbacks, there have also been times with an abundance of luck and thanks to some pretty amazing people we have made huge progress with the breed in the UK.

As a family, we now have four dogs. Alfie is our eldest. Shadow, our second dog, is mother of 22 of the dogs in the UK. You'll find more of her story in the history of the UK breed. Then there is Wilma, her story is also told later. Aristotle is one of Shadow's sons, from her first (A) litter. I wasn't supposed to keep one, but I fell in love!

DEVELOPING A BREED

What follows is a brief history of the breed development in the UK. Some is specific to the Entlebucher whilst other parts might be useful to others undertaking a similar process in other breeds.

The story started back in 2002 when Lucy Denman had the privilege of bringing the very first Entlebuchers into the country when she moved back to the UK from France bringing her dogs, Kenzo and Chloe. Kenzo and Chloe went on to have the first UK bred litter. However, none of those puppies went on to breed in the UK. Lucy made the application to have the Entlebucher recognised by the Kennel Club as a breed listed on the Import Register, which was accepted in 2006.

Over the next few years with the arrival of one or two more to the UK, the owners of those dogs started to talk to each other about the possibility of forming a club and an initial meeting did take place, but no further progress was made.

In January 2008, having not been part of those initial discussions, our family moved back to the UK from Belgium with our dog, Alfie, and made contact with the other owners. It was in April of that year that the events covered in 'My Story' unfolded and provided the determination for us to move forward.

Sometimes these things just need a different catalyst and sometimes it's just that the timing is right. This second attempt to start the Club resulted in the six founder members (Mike Caughlin, Kristina Fields, Sue Kendal, Adrianne Klijn, Chris Platt, and myself) agreeing

Queen Viktoria Spod Hradze (Queenie) at the first UK Fun Day in 2009

the principles that have remained the cornerstones of the UK Club. We would follow the Swiss model as closely as we possibly could and would seek to ensure that for the sake of the welfare of the breed we would breed to the very highest of standards, putting health at the top of our list of priorities. Those of us setting up the Club all had the same passion for the breed. We knew nothing, or at least very little! We knew no one. All we had was determination and a dream. By the time we had the key tenets of our Breeding Regulations and Club rules in place, it was 2009 thankfully by then there were others involved who knew a little more and we applied to the UK Kennel Club to be officially recognised as the UK club for the breed. That recognition was given in 2010.

In 2008 there were eight dogs registered with the Kennel Club only one of whom had the possibility of being suitable for breeding, but we had a vision.

The first UK Fun Day - Six Entlebuchers and an Australian Shepherd – Entlebuchers left to right are: Queenie, Orson, Eika, Alfie, Shadow and Guapo

Developing a breed takes luck, hard work, a touch of madness and quite a lot of money!

When the team of us who started the Club began to develop the breed in the UK, the minimum age at which a puppy could enter the country was ten months. The dog needed to have a rabies vaccination at three months, a blood test one month later and, as long as the blood showed a sufficient concentration of antibodies, could travel six months after the blood test. Ten months would be based on everything going well. It was not uncommon and happened with our eldest, Alfie, that the blood test did not show the required level of antibodies, in which case a further booster vaccination and further blood test was required with travel being postponed yet further. Once this delay had been understood it was possible to work with breeders to effectively give a two-part rabies vaccination to ensure the right level of antibodies was attained.

Needless to say, it was a challenge to find good breeders abroad who were prepared to keep a dog for this length of time and undertake the socialisation and training required. The Entlebucher needs human companionship. It is not well suited to growing up in a kennel environment and those puppies brought up in that fashion quite commonly display nervousness and temperament issues. To bring a puppy up properly for that long is expensive and therefore even if a suitable breeder could be found, the number of people willing and able to import a dog on that basis was very small.

Thankfully the changes to the Pet Passport Scheme in January 2012 made the process significantly easier. Since that date it has been possible to bring a puppy into the UK at fifteen weeks of age, which is a much better proposition.

When the Club was formed, one thing that worked very much in our favour was that no one was yet breeding from their dogs. We could therefore start by establishing best practice without upsetting the status quo. We talked to other clubs about what they wished they could change about how they went about their own development and set about learning from our colleagues in other parts of the world. Most of us who were involved at the outset knew very little, but each contributed considerably from the different knowledge we had and all were as passionate about getting it right as each other.

We set about contacting as many of the other clubs around Europe as we could find to ask them for help. Our first problem was that most of us spoke little if any German and it was a struggle to contact the right people when there was also a language barrier.

In Belgium, Alfie's breeder, Sonja van den Durpel, would help if she could. After a few months of emailing various people, I received an email from Maja Kleinjenni in Switzerland. My enquiry had been passed to her as she spoke English and she wanted to meet me to see if she felt we could work together. Asking

Flöry, Sira, Asta and Erla – Maja's dogs at my first visit in 2009

anyone to bring up a puppy for you until it is 10 months old is a lot to ask and I completely understood the need to meet me. Having developed an intense dislike of flying, I started the first of many train journeys to Switzerland and was met on the platform at Spiez by Maja and Flöry, one of her Entlebuchers. That was the point my real learning began. I spent the whole of the next few days with pen and paper asking about the Swiss breeding test, the history,

Maja's dogs, the breeding lines and absolutely everything I could think of. Maja drove me to meet breeders and dogs, including one who had been herding cattle since he was ten months old and I knew just by looking at him that he was a half-brother of my own Alfie - they could have been twins. A deep and enduring friendship had begun with Maja.

On returning to England the initial hope that the development of the breed in the UK would now be straightforward was short lived as with both the matings of Esther, Alfie's sister in Belgium, and Maja's dog, Flöry, were unsuccessful. A repeat mating for Esther resulted in only one puppy, for which there was a prior commitment and sadly that was the last litter she was able to have.

However, before Flöry had a repeat mating we received some surprising and very good news. Annette Schievenbusch, a German lady living in the UK had

agreed with an Austrian breeder to bring Akai d'Hos Moinhos d'Alvura into the UK, already in whelp. Akai would have her puppies in the UK before returning to Austria when they were ready to go to their homes. Annette contacted me to see if I knew anyone looking for puppies and of course I did... me! We went through many hurdles in trying to get the litter registered, which involved Akai herself being registered in the UK. She had four puppies, Rocky and Freddy stayed

Akai d'Hos Moinhos d'Alvura (Photo Annette Schievenbusch)

with Annette, Kai moved to Wales and the one girl from the litter, Shadow, came to live with us.

In the same year that Shadow was born, Maja found another suitable puppy for us in Switzerland. The puppy moved to live with Maja from the point at which she left her breeder at ten weeks old and we called her Megan. The plan was for me to visit regularly until she could move to England at ten months of age. When I visited her at sixteen weeks old we had a very difficult decision to make. Megan's tail was curling too far and it was unlikely she would be suitable for breeding. Much as I wanted to carry on falling in love with her, I had to take the difficult decision that she would go to a pet home and we would start the search again for a bitch that we could breed from. Thankfully, Megan went to live with her father and I've seen her a couple of times since.

We decided to wait for a puppy from Flöry. 'Megan 2' was born in the October.

Full of excitement with the news of Megan's birth, we were scheduled to attend

Victory Megan vom Kornried (Photo Maja Kleinjenni)

Discover Dogs, which is a big 'meet the breed' event in the UK. The show runs twice a year with the October event being held in London and the Kennel Club encouraging all of the recognised breeds to attend. Each breed club has a stand where there are examples of the dogs who can meet the public, while their owners can talk to those interested to learn more about the breed. With a breed which has a large population, finding enough people and dogs to represent the breed on a stand for two days is potentially not that difficult. However, when there are only a handful of the breed in the UK and they are spread across the length and breadth of the country, that is not so easy... particularly when the two dogs who are supposed to be on the stand for Saturday morning, Alfie and Shadow, had gone down with kennel cough only days before the show. As we could find no substitutes, Chris and I could be found sitting on a stand at Discover Dogs promising a dog would be along in a couple of hours. Sadly, with no dog available that was the time that TV presenter Peter Purves chose to come to get acquainted with a breed he'd never met before. He had to make do with us!

In the early days it really did seem that for every step forwards there was a similar step back. In January 2010 I set off to visit 'Megan 2' for the first time. I caught the train to London and switched station to catch the Eurostar. That was as far as I got. There were hundreds of people at St Pancras all trying to find out what was happening as sadly, due to the quantity of snow, the trains could not run. I had no choice, I turned around and went back to Kings Cross to catch the train home.

Thankfully I'd sent a blanket to Megan so she had my scent and when I finally met her at six months old she was as pleased to see me as though I'd been around all her life. That trip in April 2010 was my first visit to the Swiss Ankörung (breeding test), both to see what happened and to support Kristina Fields as she took Queenie through her test. It was a nerve-racking experience. Queenie is on the short side and was measured as being just tall enough to qualify, a great relief to all of us.

On balance, 2010 was quite a good year. Queenie's mating that summer with

Leon v. d. Auenrüti, was the first under Club rules and went according to plan, again with a lot of help from Maja. Megan moved to the UK that summer and, despite being ten months old, soon became as attached to me as our other dogs were. Queenie's litter was born in the September and again all went well.

Leon v. d. Auenrüti (Photo Serge Renggli)

The following year found me taking Shadow through her Ankörung with help from my stepson, James, whose dog she had become. Later in 2011 was my biggest saga when I took Shadow to mate for the first time. All went well with the mating and whilst she did not like standing, we had three successful trips to see Rino von der Untergass. Then we set off for home and that's when it all went wrong.

We arrived at the Eurotunnel and when we went to check her in we could not read her chip with the first microchip reader. The check-in staff found a second microchip reader and we tried again. It was at that point I was starting to realise things were not going to plan. I ran the reader over her right shoulder, her left shoulder, her right leg, and with increasing degrees of concern the rest of her body. Then I started again. They found a third reader, but by now all concerned were realising that it may not be the reader that was the problem. Eventually and with me now in a state of some distress, they gave me the details of a vet in Calais. I was travelling with my nephew on that trip and was very grateful at this point that I was not alone. My French is moderate, but at school they don't teach you the words for 'Excuse me, my dog has recently mated and may be pregnant. Now her microchip has failed and I don't know what to do.' The vet did not speak English, or at least if he did, he was not going to admit to it. He wanted to take my dog through to the surgery without me being present and without me knowing what exactly he was going to do. That was the point Shadow and I walked out.

Thankfully I am reasonably good in a crisis. It was clear I wasn't going to be travelling back to England that day, but my nephew needed to get home. Whilst we headed to find the TGV station for him to catch the Eurostar back to the UK, we worked out what the options were. Once again I knew I could get help in Belgium or Switzerland. I began the drive back to Switzerland and called Maja on the way.

Whilst an x-ray located the errant chip, the number of the chip could not be read with a scanner and so despite being only a couple of days past her mating, Shadow had to have a minor operation to remove her microchip so it could be sent back to the lab. If the lab could read the chip then I could take Shadow home. If the lab could not read the chip then, due to the old rabies

Rino v. d. Untergass (Photo Serge Renggli)

vaccination rules, Shadow would have to stay in Switzerland to have her puppies. After that, I would have to wait to take both Shadow and a whole litter of puppies back to the UK. Either way, it was not a good scenario. I had to return to England and leave Shadow in Maja's care, whilst we worked out what to do next. Everyone we turned to for assistance in Switzerland was fantastic. The pet shop even offered me a job if I wanted to stay to be with Shadow, but I had to get home.

Over the next few days I explored every avenue for bringing our dog back to England. As you can imagine my stepson was not best pleased to find his dog stranded in another country either. The only evidence of the identity of a dog that the relevant UK Government Department, DEFRA, would accept was a microchip. No matter that the University of Zurich held a sample of DNA from Shadow and could prove without doubt she was the same dog, it was the microchip or nothing. I started petitions, spoke to politicians and the media and began campaigning for our dog to come home. After two weeks the lab got in touch to say the chip could not be read. Shadow was stuck in Switzerland. Maja and I began to discuss more detailed practicalities. I would of course go to Switzerland for the birth, but after looking at the cost of hiring a vehicle big enough to transport a whole litter and the complications of registering them, we were starting to think that the best option was to move Shadow's registration to Switzerland and to find homes for her puppies there. That would have been a major blow to our plans for increasing our UK numbers.

It was a Wednesday at around 9.30am and I was driving into York. I can even tell you the exact stretch of road I was on, when my phone rang three weeks after leaving Shadow. It was the lab for the chip company. One of their technicians had continued working on the chip, even after they officially said it could not be read, and he had managed to recover the number from the chip. The paperwork could be prepared and I could bring Shadow home.

I didn't carry on driving to York that day. I turned the car around and drove straight home to pack and make arrangements for my travel. Within a day or so I was back on the road and driving to Switzerland to collect our dog.

How Shadow managed to sustain a pregnancy and give birth to seven healthy pups after the trauma she had been through, was nothing short of a miracle. The runt of the litter was Aristotle weighing just 292g and needing extra help from day one. Is it any wonder that after everything that had happened I didn't get around to finding him a home, but instead welcomed him into our family? Shadow's first born in that litter Arnold (Arnie) is named after the wonderful vet in Switzerland, Mr Odermatt, who took such good care of Shadow through the whole process.

Shadow and the Torfheide A litter

In 2012 it was back to Switzerland for my third Ankörung, this time with Megan and to support Annie and Aida and their owners Vanessa Oakes and Martha Maguire. Shadow's trip for her second mating later that year was thankfully uneventful, if you discount an unfortunate incident leaving me having to drive for an hour with my trouser leg coated in semen and related bodily fluids from the stud dog! Thankfully Queenie's mating that year went smoothly too.

From just after a few hours after their birth, Shadow's second litter was televised 24 hours a day on an internet tv channel. Footage included everything from my cleaning out the pen while still in my pyjamas to the more photogenic puppies growing up. Other than it being a wonderful way for the new owners to

Aida and Annie Norfolkfields (Photo Serge Renggli)

watch their own puppies, it turned out to be the most watched litter the tv channel had broadcast to that point. On the downside, at least one of the puppies needed a night-light when he went to his new home as he wasn't used to the dark, due to my leaving a light on for the camera to work.

Whilst much of 2012 went to plan, that was not true when we came to mate Megan. Her first trip was to the Netherlands and she had a split season with her progesterone level dropping after we'd set off, before then starting to climb again. I stayed in the Netherlands as long as I could and she did mate on the last day before I had to leave. Sadly, it did not result in a pregnancy. In the autumn when mating Shadow, Megan travelled with me and despite not being due, her season started early. We decided that it made sense to mate her with a Swiss dog as we were already there and based on the past performance thought that it would be at least a week before she was ready. I would leave her in Switzerland and come back seven to ten days later once she had mated and was ready to come home. This time her progesterone level shot up, instead of taking a long time to rise and I had only got as far as the Club's Southern Fun Day on my way home, when I got a call to say she had already mated. I went to the supermarket in Maidenhead and bought clean underwear and tee shirts and the morning after the Fun Day I drove back to Switzerland to collect her. Sadly, once again Megan did not become pregnant.

As the Club continued to grow and develop and others with their new pups became heavily involved in activities, 2013 saw me take up studying both genetics and German. I realised if I was going to make any real progress then these were both areas of which I needed to have a much better understanding. Four years on and I'm still studying German and am still not desperately good at it. I made better progress in gaining a basic understanding of genetics and now have at least enough knowledge to make sense of some of the things I need to read.

Megan was mated twice more in 2013 before going to a specialist who concluded that for several reasons she was not going to become pregnant. You can take 'dog most like its owner' a step too far!

Artus v. oberen Dorfberg – father of Queenie's B litter (Photo Serge Renggli)

Despite losing Megan from the breeding programme, 2013 was a good year. The Kennel Club agreed the Interim Breed Standard in the UK meaning for the first time the dogs could be shown here. We also started to find some good imports to bring into the country to boost our numbers and start to widen our gene pool. It was also the first time the Club held its own Ankörung (breeding test) meaning dogs no longer had to travel abroad to be tested. In turn this meant that Eiger (Norfolkfields Benji) qualified as the first UK stud dog, although to date he is still waiting for a suitable UK match.

2014 was another year of firsts for the Club. We ran our first Judge Training Course, to prepare those who judge the breed to have a better understanding of what they should be looking for. As a breed, our first dogs qualified for Crufts and appeared in the show ring there. Also in that year the first litter of 'second generation' puppies was born, when Norfolkfields Annie gave birth to four pups of her own.

Shadow's final litter was another complicated affair. The first mating for this litter was in winter. More to the point it involved spending Christmas in Switzerland while leaving the rest of my family in England, temperatures of minus seventeen Celsius, the car breaking down, walking into the low hanging eaves of a building and giving myself concussion and no resulting pregnancy for the dog! In fairness, Switzerland is incredibly beautiful at this time of year and I was made very welcome, so it was not a wasted trip, but things could have gone more smoothly. The repeat mating six months later was, despite very high temperatures and struggling to keep Shadow cool in the hotel, a complete success.

Guapo (Photo Mike Caughlin)

By this stage we had had our first losses of dogs through old age, with the original UK litter having reached the end of their lives as well as Guapo who had arrived as an import a little later. Guapo, together with his owner Mike Caughlin, had been a very important part of the setup of the Club.

In 2015 I imported a new puppy, Wilma, for breeding, only to find when she was entered in her first dog show, that as she had grown her jaw had become slightly undershot. Sadly, this made it unlikely that she would pass her breeding test. It is not a common problem in the breed, but as a potential genetic defect it would be unwise to pass it on. As a breeder, with the best will in the world, you cannot predict when things like this will occur. Wilma has a most remarkable temperament and is now my constant companion.

In 2016 we celebrated the Club's first all UK mating. It was planned with the same care as all the others and yet still produced our first seriously ill puppy, Heidi, who has a condition known as ectopic ureter. Some of the proceeds of this book will go to help pay for her care and further treatment. One of her litter mates had a serious heart problem, which was thankfully successfully operated on. Sometimes luck just isn't on your side.

Other than those setbacks, the years 2015 to 2017 have seen the breed grow to 92 dogs in the UK, with healthy happy puppies born in the UK and imports from abroad joining our numbers. As a Club we're looking forward to reaching the milestone of 100 dogs and that will be a big cause for celebration.

Wilma v. Rickental Crufts 2017 (Photo Lizz Alexander)

We've learned a lot along the way. Our puppy application process is strict and thankfully that has led to relatively few dogs being rehomed over the years. As a Club we try to provide lifelong support to all our dogs, and their owners, to make sure they get the best out of life. We've discovered that however much we do know, there's an awful lot we still don't know and it's a constant learning curve. We have come to understand both the importance of widening the gene pool and, and the difficulty of doing so when you live on an island with very few of the breed. Keeping our breed standard in line with the one used internationally is a very important part of being able to do this.

On a personal level I have learned a huge amount - some genetics, some German, and the fact that there are no shortcuts if you are going to get it right. I've also learned as a responsible breeder you rarely make any money out of breeding. I've learned just how much hard work developing a breed can take. I have appreciated the support of a husband who copes with some very peculiar changes of plan and not knowing where I will be from day to day. I have also appreciated the close knit and supportive Entlebucher community, both in the UK and abroad, who are equally passionate about the breed and work so hard to ensure its continued health and welfare.

Finally, and above anything else, I have learned to always check the microchip!

Purpose

The key to understanding many of the behaviours of the breed is to consider their purpose and what they have been bred for. It is incredible how many behavioural as well as physical traits are deeply coded into the DNA of the dog. It should not be surprising to us that in certain circumstances it is their instincts which in the first instance will guide behaviour. As a human you only have to think about your own natural reaction on seeing something such as a snake to realise that we too respond to some situations in a particular manner without having to be taught.

Historically, the Entlebucher was a herding dog and still is in some places today. As an Alpine herder he would spend many months working closely with the herdsman in the mountainous summer pastures. At home his, or more likely her, job would be to keep the farm free from vermin. The dogs were also used to pull a small cart with a milk churn to the dairy.

Glenn vom Kornried has been herding cattle since about 10 months of age (Photo Serge Renggli)

If you think that an Entlebucher weighs at most 30kg and a cow may be between 500kg and 750kg you start to get the picture of the scale of the job in hand. The dog must be 'fearless'. It has to not only stand up to cows, but keep them together and get them to move in the direction the herdsman wants them to go. Whilst only a dog properly trained to herd should be allowed around farm animals, an untrained one will still exhibit many of the instinctive behaviours. He will run around his humans when outdoors making sure they keep together. He may also do this around the house. Nothing is more problematic to an Entlebucher when out on a walk than his party of humans splitting and going in two different directions. It will take him some while to cease to be convinced he needs to do something about it and act on his own initiative.

Simply running around is not enough to move a stubborn cow. The dog is not in a position to reason with the cow and persuade them to move by discussion, so given the disparity in size they have two approaches open to them. Firstly, they will nip at the side or heel of the animal to convince them to do what they are being asked. They don't break the skin, but a cow is big and strong and it can take a sharp nip to get it to react. At home the Entlebucher needs to remember that you are the herdsman and not the herd and training in bite inhibition is very important as part of this. Even then in moments of high excitement the dog may 'forget'. In my own most embarrassing experience my dog, Megan, chose the first exercise in her Gold Good Citizen exam as the moment to disagree with a command and go for her instinctive approach. We failed! As a result of this however, I learned a great deal about managing her in those situations and the need for a 'time out' for an overexcited dog to be able to calm down and be able to focus.

The second behaviour that is used can be just as effective and equally painful, especially when you don't see it coming. The Entlebucher has a remarkable ability to jump from an almost standing start and body-slam using his full body weight.

Torfheide Beethoven at Skyeannroos (Basil) (Photo Robyn Burnett)

When this is against half a tonne of cow I'm sure it is very helpful, but it can be a bit of a bruising surprise for a human. Owners never cease to be amazed at just how high these dogs can jump.

Keeping the farm free of vermin is another trait they bring into their home environment. In my personal experience this is a trait more evident amongst bitches than dogs. If you have other family pets then their introduction to an Entlebucher needs to be a careful one and is easiest while the dog is a puppy. I do know of dogs who help to round up the family hens, live in harmony with pet rabbits and are best friends with the cat. However, I have also been brought offerings of dead garden birds and had to return a baby rabbit to the pet shop for its own safety after my dog, Alfie, normally a mild-mannered sort, became utterly fixated on getting to the rabbit at any cost. The same dog exhibited a similar alarming reaction to a very small and rat-like toy breed dog on another occasion - a behaviour which seemed utterly out of character in a loving family pet, but has its roots in much more instinctive past requirements.

For pulling a milk churn on a cart, sometimes unaccompanied, there are a number of characteristics which are required. Firstly, the dog must be strong - and they are. The best way we have found to demonstrate this to would-be owners is to give them the lead of one of our male dogs and then for me to walk away. Because the dog is so keen to be with me, and I'll come back to that in a minute, he will pull with all his strength and the prospective owner can see what they might be up against. To be fair, it is unusual for an Entlebucher to want to pull away from his own human unless under specific instruction, but it helps to understand their sheer power.

The fact that they sometimes go on their own with the churn is also important. These dogs are independent thinking. They can evaluate and react to situations and will think about what they should do. For my own part, I love having dogs who are that intelligent. It keeps me on my toes. For new owners it is critical to stress the importance of training the dog before the dog trains you.

I have left until last the trait that is the one which above all makes them such a wonderful animal to live

Wilma and Shadow dreaming of cart pulling times!

with. Due to the time they have spent over the years in close one to one relationships with their herdsman, they develop a very strong attachment to their prime carer. I have heard it described as a 'pathological' attachment, which is fair comment. They really cannot help themselves getting that close to you. Of course, they are not all the same and some are far more balanced than others, but it is not an exaggeration to say that most Entlebuchers I know would be happy if they could spend 24 hours a day with at least some part of them physically touching their human. They lean against your legs if you are on a chair and they are not, or on top of you if you allow them on the chair. They will follow you around the house, including to the bathroom and would probably even get in the shower with you if you gave them the chance. If you want a dog that you can leave without human company for hours then buy the stuffed toy version available from Ikea,

but if you want a dog who will never tire of your company and will be as faithful and loyal as any dog could be, then there is no greater dog than an Entlebucher Mountain Dog.

As a footnote to that, their purpose has historically meant being outdoors a great deal and they do love being outside, but generally not if you don't go with them. They would rather be wherever you are. Also, whilst they come alive when it snows and show sheer delight, in general they much prefer to go out on a sunny day than a cold windy day in England!

THE FOUR SWISS MOUNTAIN DOG BREEDS

Leaving aside the St Bernard, which has been recognised as a distinct breed for several centuries, there are four Swiss Mountain Dog Breeds.

The four are closely related, have very similar markings, but do differ in a number of other respects.

The Great Swiss is the largest of the four, standing up to 72cm at the shoulder. He is short-haired and heavy boned. He can weigh about twice as much as an Entlebucher but is temperamentally not dissimilar, although less lively and agile. His proportions differ a little to the Entlebucher, being not quite so long in the body compared to his height and with a squarer head. Although he was identified as a separate breed before the Entlebucher, a breed standard was not agreed for the breed until 1939.

Great Swiss Mountain Dog (Photo Ute Rüegg)

Bernese Mountain Dog (Photo Ute Rüegg)

The Bernese Mountain Dog is the only long-haired dog in the family. He was originally known as a Dürrbächler after a small area where he was commonly found. He was known as a Bernese or Berner Sennenhund from 1910. He stands a couple of centimetres shorter than the Great Swiss, but with similar proportions of height to length and although the long hair makes him look large, he weighs around 10kg less than the Great Swiss with a maximum of about 50kg. He has the shortest life expectancy of the four Swiss Mountain Dog breeds. He also needs significantly more grooming.

The third in the family is the Appenzeller. The Appenzell Cattle Dog or

Appenzeller (Photo Ute Rüegg)

Appenzeller Sennenhund, was the earliest of the four breeds to be officially recognised. Named after the region in the east of Switzerland where his development took place, the Appenzeller was described in 1853 as being "high-pitch barking, short-haired, medium size, multicolour cattle dog of a quite even Spitz type…" He stands taller than an Entlebucher at up to 56cm at the shoulder and has the squarer shape of the larger breeds in the family. The other two key differences in observation are that the tail of an Appenzeller is expected to curl around, which led to him being likened to the 'Spitz' type, and it is permissible for his main colour to be a dark brown.

The Entlebucher is the smallest cousin. In character he has most in common with the Bernese and Great Swiss, although he is more wary of strangers. He is of course described in detail throughout this book.

OWNING AN ENTLEBUCHER

Buying and owning any dog is expensive and an Entlebucher is no exception. As the breed is not a common one it can also mean a long wait for a suitable puppy. Occasionally there are opportunities to take a rehomed adult, but that is not something to undertake lightly. Consideration should be given to the reason for the rehoming and the skills the new owner has available to manage any difficulties. There can be reasons for a well behaved and well-balanced dog to be rehomed, but equally it can be due to the relationship between dog and human breaking down. Where the latter is the case, then a new owner is more likely to be successful if they are experienced in dog handling and training and have the time to devote to help the dog to achieve his potential. Also, when rehoming a dog, consideration needs to be given to the age of the dog and any particular challenges this may bring. If the dog is going through a challenging phase, such as teenage, then the settling period will be more difficult than with a fully mature adult.

Mother and child

As a Club, we have received comments that our application for a puppy is more like an adoption process than taking on a puppy. There's a reason for that. Taking on a dog of any age is very like an adoption and every effort must be made to make sure it is a good match for all parties. Rehoming a dog because it has not worked out for them first time around is not something any breeder wants to see happen. When a puppy goes to his home, a breeder wants nothing but the best for their puppy for their whole life. Crazy as it might make me sound, before any of our puppies has left I have whispered a little promise to him that wherever he is, and whatever the problem, all he has to do is call and I'll be there. It's a promise I will always keep.

Owning a dog is a commitment for the whole of that dog's life. The cost of a puppy may seem high, but it is very small when compared to the lifetime cost of food / medical treatment / insurance etc. It is not something to enter into lightly.

As I have explained in the section on the breed's purpose, Entlebuchers are very bright, intelligent dogs who form an exceptionally close bond with their prime carer and who would defend their family to the last. Although wary of strangers they are quick to welcome any new person confirmed as a member of their pack and are very good with children. They are not a dog to suit a person or family who expects to be away from them for long periods of time on a regular basis, as they thrive on human contact and their need for mental stimulation can prove difficult to manage if they are left to their own devices. However, their intelligence does make them fast learners and they enjoy any new opportunities.

They are best suited to cold or temperate climates and their dense undercoat can make it difficult for them to adapt to really hot temperatures. They are never happier than when they see snow and will romp, leaving no doubt that they were born to it.

Whilst strong and assertive, at no time should an Entlebucher

Isone and Sina (Photo Ute Rüegg)

be aggressive. That should not be confused with their preparedness to defend their pack if it were ever needed. I have no doubt that any one of my dogs would die for me if he or she thought I was being directly threatened, rather than leave me at risk. However, on the occasions when I have seen any of them go into a protective stance, in the first instance they do so more politely than you would imagine possible. On one occasion a five-year-old human member of our dog's pack was engaged in a play sword fight with a larger and much older human cousin, who the dog, Alfie, had not previously met. Alfie went and sat very conspicuously between the five-year-old and his cousin as much as to say, 'If you want to take him on, then you have to deal with me first.' There was no mistaking his intention, but he gave only the mildest of warning growls and simply stood, or more to the point sat, his ground.

Owning an Entlebucher is a privilege and with the investment of time and energy to train the dog, an owner will have a relationship that will bring many hours of happiness. Make no mistake, these dogs are bright and need to be trained.

If they are the one in charge, then you will have many hours of stress rather than pleasure. They do not respond well to heavy handedness, but earn their respect by gentle, consistent and firm leadership and they will give you their devotion and total dedication in return. Staying one step ahead of them can be a challenge as, unlike many breeds, they are very capable of problem solving. Whether they apply their skills to dismantling a crate or going to any length to retrieve something they have lost, or you have placed out of reach, they will sooner or later work out what to do. I always joke that I can't leave Aristotle for too long because he's so bright he'd have sold the house and moved the money offshore before I got back. That may of course be a slight exaggeration, but I wouldn't put it past him.

Taking Your Puppy Home

Torfheide Bosanova (Tucker) about to catch the train to his new home

From the point you leave the breeder's home, your puppy will be dependent on you for everything. With your help, he can grow into a happy outgoing and well-mannered dog. His transition will be made much easier if you have spent time with him, getting to know him, before you take him home. Where it is not practical for this to take place, you should buy a suitable 'comforter' or blanket - the softer and snugglier the better, and sleep with it under your arm for several nights. Ideally the same should be done by all the key members of the puppy's new pack, including other dogs etc. This blanket should then be sent to the breeder so that your pup can spend time with your scent long before he comes to live with you. Over time, not only will be feel he has got to know a little about you, but the scents of his breeder and dog

26

family will be picked up on the blanket and work in reverse when he leaves to live with you, giving comfort when away from his breeder's home.

The first question on most owners' minds is 'What do I need to have considered for the journey to take my puppy home?' Of course, it will depend on how you are travelling and how far you have to go, but if your puppy has not yet had all his vaccinations then it is important to remember you should not get him out in public areas where other, potentially unvaccinated, dogs have been. He should not yet be walking on the pavement, or getting out of the car at a service station for example.

Torfheide Cinderella getting used to her new harness ready to be put in the car to go home

You will need a collar, which fits the neck size of the puppy. It is very important if you plan to attach a lead to the collar that the collar fits comfortably, but is not too loose. The collar should have a tag on it with all the necessary details for the puppy. In the UK that means the name and address, including post code, of the owner. It is also wise to include a phone number for more immediate contact and, on the reverse, your vet's phone number, in case of emergency. My own preference is for the dog to have a harness for the lead to attach to. I find the breed respond very well to wearing a harness and it has the added advantage that a dog car seat belt can be attached to the harness clip for secure car travel.

If you are travelling by car then a seat belt or crate will provide safety for the dog. Getting him used to travelling in this way from day one is worthwhile. Crates are available for most sizes of car boot, but consideration must also be given to there being adequate room for the dog to move about and be comfortable. If you are travelling by train or other public transport, then a lightweight crate which can be carried will be the best option, but bear in mind that at eight weeks old your puppy will already weigh around 5 - 6kg. You can buy dog rucksacks to carry your pup in. These strap to the front of the body with a clip to attach to the puppy's harness for safety. You can buy ones which will take weight up to 10 - 12kg and they can be very useful for carrying your puppy in early socialisation, before he is fully vaccinated.

Very often a pup will sleep for most of a car or train journey of a few hours. However, having an old towel or puppy pads under him will help if he does need the toilet while travelling. Also make sure you have with you fresh water and a bowl and, if the journey is longer, enough food for his meals. Having his comforter with him is also a good idea as well as a soft toy and something harder that he can chew.

Ready for him at home, he should have his own bed and a crate if that is something you plan to use. He will need food and water bowls and some toys.

The First Night

Every new owner worries about the first night. This will be the first time your pup

*Torfheide Cinderella ready for her first night
(Photo Lucy Heath)*

has been away from his mum and litter mates and been on his own. His breeder should have given him some experience of time on his own, but it is hard to prepare him for the changes which take place when he leaves the nest. What you do now will set the pattern for the weeks to come. If the pup is sleeping on his own, he is very likely to cry on his first night. If his human goes to him to provide comfort, then he will very soon learn an effective pattern of behaviour. Cry - response. Cry - response. Within days, the human will be tired and frustrated and wondering how they will ever get their puppy to settle.

There is a big difference between crying for attention and crying in real distress. Sometimes you have to be cruel to be kind. In the same way as you would with a child, if the puppy is simply seeking attention, if you ignore the cry then he will very soon settle. However, if the puppy is genuinely distressed, which can be for many reasons including needing to go to the toilet, then ignoring him is not the answer. When he is very young then he may not be able to go for a full eight-hours without needing the toilet. If you want him to sleep in another room then a baby monitor can be a very good way of hearing when he wakes up and needs to be taken out.

Early Days

The early days can be challenging as a new owner is often uncertain if they are doing things 'right'. Here are a few points which may help:

Nutrition - feed the puppy a good puppy food. If you opt for a kibble there will be a feeding guide on the packet. The amount given is usually expressed in a daily amount for each stage of the pup's development. This is then split between the number of meals the pup is being given - it is not usually a per meal amount. Do read the pack carefully. Also check the weight of your pup and his age against the packet on a regular basis, as the feeding amount will change as the pup grows - first increasing and then decreasing again once the pup has done most of his growing. If you are feeding the correct amount then you do not need to feed an excessive level of treats on top. Use some of pup's food as training treats etc. rather than overfeeding him.

Rest - a puppy needs to rest. He should have a place he feels safe and is undisturbed. If there are children in the house then they may need to be kept away from the puppy at the times the puppy needs a nap, unless they can be supervised to nap together. As you watch the puppy day by day, there will be days he looks very fat in the middle and then a day where he sleeps and suddenly it is as though someone rolled him out and he is longer in the body and leg. This cycle repeats itself as the puppy continues to grow.

Safety - your pup needs his environment to be safe. He will be inquisitive. If things are at ground level or easily reached / pulled off - he will investigate. Keep anything which is dangerous to the pup (medicines / sharp objects / things he should not

Torfheide Annette (Soggeli) and Aristotle exploring

chew etc.) out of his reach at all times!

Toys - these do not have to be the latest or the most expensive. Homemade toys can work just as well. An old plastic bottle, either empty or partially filled with water or stones and the lid securely fitted, can keep him occupied for hours. Do check regularly for damage as in time the bottle may become punctured. Even an empty bottle can be fun, if you don't want to risk the mess! A cardboard inner from a kitchen roll can give endless fun. Previously filled bones or Kong toys refilled with combinations of banana, plain yoghurt, kibble, carrot etc. and then frozen, can not only entertain the pup, but also help him with teething as he both chews and soothes his mouth on

Torfheide Alan (Rafa)

the chilled contents. Look online for toys you can make. There are some great ideas.

Day to Day Health - take your pup for a vet check within a couple of days of coming home. This also introduces him to the veterinary surgery at a time when treatment is not required and he does not have to associate it with stress. Discuss with your vet the timings of vaccinations including kennel cough (usually annual), worming (quarterly), flea and tick treatment (varies according to option being used). Keep all routine medical protection up to date.

Bed - choose something hard wearing, which is also easy to keep clean. A surprising number of pet beds disintegrate when put through a wash process or are impossible to get the cover back on after washing. Your dog does not need a 'fashion bed'; that is more about you the owner than the aesthetic tastes of your dog. A bed which makes him feel warm, safe and comfortable is what your dog will appreciate. If you get one with an extra base cushion don't be offended if the dog digs that up and rearranges things to his liking! He may even prefer to use the cushion as a pillow.

Most importantly, enjoy every minute of those early days as they pass all too quickly.

Puppyhood

Socialisation of your puppy is very important. An Entlebucher should be inquisitive and fearless. That does not happen without support. All dogs go through a number of 'fear stages'. Not only is it important to expose them to as many experiences as possible prior to these stages, but it is essential to support them as they go through those stages. I have found that in general when a young Entlebucher shows a fear reaction, if the human they trust takes them up to the item or situation which has caused concern and shows them it's ok, then they relax and are fine. If you ignore their fear and do not help them to realise it is groundless then the fear will remain. It can happen in all sorts of situations, from an empty plant pot suddenly being blown at them by the wind, to a noise suddenly starting which they were not expecting.

You have a responsibility to think ahead. Try not to take them into situations during a fear stage which are almost certainly going to cause concern. It's easy to do so inadvertently and can take a lot of work to put right. It was cold outside, so I started the car engine to warm the car before going for a walk. I then expected one of my dogs, who was going through her final fear stage, to jump into the car. This meant jumping over where the noisy, smelly exhaust pipe was pumping out fumes. The upshot was several weeks of work to make her happy to jump into the

Wilma's first train travel

boot of the car, even when the engine was not running. If I had thought about it from her point of view, I could have avoided the problem. You might laugh at the idea of thinking like a dog, but it is a very useful technique. Look at situations as though you were at their height off the ground, can see what is in their range of vision and no more, but might be able to hear

and smell things that a human is less sensitive to. If you have ever tried to lead a small child through a crowd where all they can see is knees and legs and where people walk into them because they don't look down, you will start to get an idea of what a similar situation is like for your dog.

Sometimes situations are unfortunate. A high-pitched noise from a hearing-aid has left my dog, Wilma, unwilling to go to the person who was wearing it. They don't forget!

Aristotle meeting Santa Claus

Expose them to as many and as varied situations as possible when they are young, but always from the safety of them seeing you there and you being relaxed. If you are stressed they will be very quick to pick up on it. This is particularly important for owners who have situations they are not comfortable with. Ideally find another close human pack member to expose the pup to those situations, so they don't pick up on your fears and become conditioned by them.

If you find a situation they don't react well to, try to understand their point of view and see if you can work out what is bothering them. Wilma is slightly claustrophobic and I've learned that on a train it is best to only get up and get ready to get off when the doors open and not go to stand in the small cramped doorway waiting. Similarly, this is a breed that is not keen on strangers. On the train Wilma is happy if we are on forward facing airline style seats where she can sit under the seat at my feet, but never happy in seats which face people that she does not know. Presented with that situation it can take a lot of treats and games to keep her attention on me and to stop her barking. It's little different from trying to take a small child's mind off something they don't like.

Don't underestimate what can be seen as different. Beards, hair colour, glasses, skin colour, rucksacks, hats, bicycles, wheelchairs, crutches, stiletto heels, heavy boots, screaming children, thunder, falling leaves, cats, traffic, heavy rain on an umbrella, extractor fans, car horns… can all give a dog pause for thought. Your job is to make sure your dog knows they are all just everyday occurrences and nothing to be alarmed by.

The first fear stage can start as early as five to six weeks of age, so it is essential to make sure your pup comes from a good breeder who will take the time to get the puppy used to as many things as possible before he even comes to you. There are very good downloads of a range of noises which can be played to the pups to get them used to noise. They should have different stimulating toys, different surfaces to walk on, and different people and dogs to meet. They should also learn to spend time on their own at this stage. A good breeder will give their puppies a strong foundation for their new family to build on.

Something to remember is that one of the purposes around the farm was for an Entlebucher to dispose of vermin. They have a prey drive for small fury things. I've known this extend to very small dogs that look more like vermin, so be careful. If you have rabbits, chickens, cats or canaries then introduce the puppy to them as young as possible and in a controlled fashion. No one is going to be happy with the puppy if it reduces the family pet numbers. With training, an Entlebucher will accept all these into his pack.

Introduce puppies to other adult dogs - Torfheide Beija meeting Alfie

Some Entlebuchers have a greater prey drive than others so if you are going to be keeping your puppy with small animals then talk to the breeder about the parents of the pup and start socialisation as early as possible. I had to stop feeding the garden birds to stop our dog, Shadow, from lying in wait for innocent victims and, much like a cat, bringing them to me as presents.

Toilet training an Entlebucher is generally fairly straightforward. They want to be clean and they want to make their humans happy. Given the choice between getting it right and getting it wrong they will almost always choose right, as long as they understand what their humans expect or want. You should however note that a puppy does not have fully developed bladder muscles and control. Accidents will happen. Do not get cross with a puppy for this. The first thing as a human is to ask yourself whether the accident occurred because you didn't react to the needs of your puppy at the right time. Initially take the puppy outside to where you want him to go to the toilet every half an hour. Choose a command to use that he will associate with toiletting. Find something that is not embarrassing. You'll thank me later! I use 'Go'. You can build up from half an hour in stages when you are happy that things are going well. Add an extra quarter of an hour each time and before long the interval will be reasonably long. Always at this stage go out of the same door. In no time at all the puppy will go to that door when he wants to go out. You still need to be alert. If he sits there quietly then you need to realise he is there and not forget him. If you do forget, then don't blame the puppy

when you have to clear up. Of course, you don't need to wake a sleeping puppy to take him out, but as soon as he wakes up it is the very first thing you must do, so again you as the human need to be alert. Owners who expect to be able to leave their puppy for several hours at a time when the puppy is young and then wonder why the dog is not toilet trained only have themselves to blame.

The great thing if he will go to the toilet on command is that when you are travelling you can get him out of the car, toiletted and carry on with the journey with the minimum of disruption. In heavy rain that is always a bonus.

When I said above that they will 'almost always choose to get it right', I have had a situation of a dog, in this case Alfie, having been told off for something completely different, very deliberately and in full knowledge of what he was doing, walk over to a full basket of clean washing and cock his leg over it. You have been warned! These dogs are bright.

Playing 'tug' with a toy or rope might be fun, but remember that this is instinctively a game about pack order. If they win, then there are implications in how they see themselves within the family structure. Teach the dog to let go when you say so and that the game finishes on your command. Whilst they may be very clear that you are their pack leader, this will not extend to every member of the household. If you allow children to play 'rough and tumble' with a small ten-week-old puppy, because it seems fun, don't be surprised when you have 25kg of solid muscle that is too rough with the children, who have not grown at the same rate, and now don't know how to handle him.

If you give a pup a 'toy' shoe to play with, don't be surprised when he does not recognise the difference between this one and ones you were hoping to wear again. They may be bright, but don't set your dog up to fail.

When a small child is teething, we give him a teething ring so that he can soothe the discomfort and help the teeth come through. Your puppy will go through the same thing. Have something suitable handy to put in his

Alfie teaching Shadow to play

mouth when he starts looking for something to chew for that purpose. If you don't provide something appropriate he will find something for himself and it would be unfair to complain that he chose the wrong thing.

Puppyhood sets a dog up for life. The boundaries you set now will be key to behaviours later.

Terrible Twos

Puppies go through many of the same developmental stages as children. Of course, once you take into account the age of maturity of a dog compared with a human, you realise the process is somewhat condensed. The 'terrible twos' in which your 'toddler' first starts to exercise his independence and discover what he is capable of, in an Entlebucher occurs at around six months of age. For a matter of a few weeks he will push the boundaries and try your patience to the limit. He will apparently forget everything he has learned to date and go back to being a fairly unruly puppy. This is normal.

This is the time to stay firm, focussed and consistent. It is a relatively short phase and at the end of it, as long as he has not been left to run wild, he will suddenly remember his manners and go back to being the lovely puppy you thought you were getting to know. He will remember the training he has had and start to follow some instructions again.

However frustrating a puppy's behaviour is in this time, you will get further through positive reinforcement of good behaviour and being patient but firm in insisting your standards are met, than you ever will do by getting cross. In the same way as with a human child, be prepared to count to ten, a hundred, a thousand, whatever it takes. Funnily enough, I think my dogs all learned the numbers one to ten and knew by the last one they really needed to comply. They often pushed it to nine and three-quarters before doing what had been asked, though!

Teenage

As with human children, a dog will go through a 'teenage' phase. This is when

Teenagers at play - Wilma v. Rickental and Corbin-Bernie Loch Ranch – both 18 months old

their hormones are really starting to fully function and their body is beginning to become mature. Like any teenager, they will think they rule the world. They think they know everything and you know nothing. They will test every boundary, answer back and push the limits of behaviour. They will pretend they know none of the good behaviours they have learned in class and around the home. They will try your patience to the limits, pulling on the lead once again, running off and not returning when called. They will find every opportunity to embarrass you. This stage usually starts at between about 15 months and 18 months of age and can last for a few months. Thankfully, it is short lived, however it can be nonetheless difficult and depending on what happens during that time can either leave you with the sweetest adult dog or a real handful.

This is not the time to leave your dog's training to chance. Be consistent. Be clear. Reward good behaviours and gently but firmly correct inappropriate behaviour. This is often when two particular behaviours can kick in and I have dealt with them separately in the 'Common Issues' section. The first of these behaviours is barking. An Entlebucher who has been very quiet may commonly find his voice around now. This can make group training classes difficult, particularly if you have a trainer who is not familiar with the breed. The second is their inherent drive to protect you against people they do not know. Combined with their natural wariness of strangers this can be hard to handle and does need to be managed so it does not become a problem.

Torfheide Aristotle

Just at the point you think that teenage will last forever, you will find that the dog who wakes up is not the same dog as you had the day before and they will start to mellow into a responsible adult.

If you are struggling with any particular behaviour, turning to a more experienced Entlebucher owner who has already been through this stage will pay dividends. A breed specific expert is often of significantly more use in helping you through behaviours common to the breed than a general behaviourist who is unfamiliar with the breed's foibles.

Adulthood

An Entlebucher is fully physically mature by around two years of age. Mentally, he may pretend otherwise and some seem to maintain a puppy outlook for a good while longer, but they all get there in their own time.

A three or four-year-old Entlebucher is a dog in his prime. These are days to savour. Physically he is both mature and beautiful to behold. Watching him run is a sight to enjoy. He will be your most faithful friend and companion and his intelligence and ingenuity will give you hours of pleasure. He should by now be happy to wait quietly while you do other things and not demand attention at those times. However, he will always have one eye on you and be ready at a moment's notice to join in whatever the next activity is.

He may not be as cute as the puppy you brought home, but he will be more rewarding than ever and it is now that all the work you put in while he was young will really pay off.

He will be in tune with your every mood and always try to comfort you if you show distress. There will still be times he is a handful and he may get overexcited in certain situations, but he will be relaxed, happy and obedient most of the time. Don't be surprised if his obedience is a little delayed. They have a tendency to think through whether they want to comply before getting on with what's

Kuno v. Frutigen (Photo Serge Renggli)

required. However, if you set him a 'job' whether that is swimming lengths at the pool or carrying a load, he will take the request very seriously and be deterred by nothing.

Old Age

Most dog food manufacturers place dogs in the 'Senior' category from seven years. No one told that to an Entlebucher. Many Entlebuchers would be insulted at that suggestion. By the age of seven in general they will be as willing to play ball and run around as any younger dog and remain lively and energetic long past this age. If you change his diet too soon, don't be surprised when he starts to raid the bin and seek alternative food sources.

Of course, if he has been injured you may need to restrict his exercise, but otherwise moving him to a lower energy food makes little sense. What these 'Senior' foods do include are joint supplements and vitamin support that can be

Einstein van de Tiendenschuur (Alfie) at 12 years old

beneficial as a dog ages. It is important to make sure he is getting all of this from whatever you do feed your dog. More important is to monitor his weight. As with humans, it is all too easy to start putting on a few extra pounds and with it will come more pressure on joints and additional strains that are unnecessary. I've heard owners argue that the amount of food they are giving their dog 'just doesn't seem very much'. Of course it doesn't by human standards, but they aren't the size of humans. Even a very small human is about twice the weight of a large, fit

Entlebucher. If you are feeding them a quality food then hopefully they will get all they need from it, without the need for wide ranging 'treats'.

An elderly Entlebucher is a very beautiful sight. They go grey with a dignity and a distinguished look that I can only envy as a human. The gentleness of the eyes tells a soulful story and they will want nothing more than to be close to your side and to receive the same tenderness and affection you showered on their younger selves. It is also important to run your hands over your dog regularly to ensure any lumps and bumps, aches and pains which may appear can be picked up at an early stage and treated if necessary.

By around nine or ten years of age an Entlebucher may slow down just a little.

Charley

More likely, they forget to slow down and wake up after a good romp a little stiffer than they might prefer. It is not unusual by this stage for them to have a little arthritis, especially in sites of previous injury. A regular swim for the dog can help to keep joints moving freely and is very well worthwhile.

The life expectancy of an Entlebucher is usually quoted as being between eleven and thirteen years. Thankfully, I've known a good number pass these ages and even reach their sixteenth or seventeenth birthdays. Those are rare however, and most reach the end of their natural lives in the range stated. As they get older you learn to treasure each day and do what you can to ease the aches and pains they develop. They need just as much love as they ever did and will give their own love in return.

Feeding

A puppy will normally have 4 meals a day from weaning until he is twelve to fourteen weeks of age. If he is clearing the bowl constantly then increase meals as required, but be careful because some puppies are just greedy. It is better for their growth to be slow and steady as this will lead to stronger better formed joints. Do not leave unfinished food down for a puppy. Most good dog foods provide guidance on the correct measure of food according to the age and weight of the puppy. This is usually written as an amount per day which can then be split between the appropriate number of meals.

Most importantly leave a bowl of fresh water at all times. A puppy's drinking requirements vary. However, if your puppy seems to be drinking excessive quantities, it is worth consulting your vet to ensure it is not a sign of infection.

From three months to six months, three meals a day should be sufficient. Very often a dog will tell you when he is ready to cut down on the frequency of eating by regularly leaving one meal almost untouched. That does not usually stop him begging for what you are eating or any other food left lying around!

Torfheide A Litter - early attempt at solids

From six months onwards, the dog is normally ready to reduce to two meals a day. Good times are breakfast and tea-time. Feed the recommended amount for the age and weight of your puppy according to the food manufacturer's guidelines. You should check these regularly to make sure that the amount is still appropriate. Once the dog has stopped growing as rapidly, the amount he needs reduces. A good method of checking that your dog is not overweight is to see if you can feel his ribs. You should not have to sink your fingers into layers of 'puppy fat', nor should you be able to see his ribs sticking out.

If you change your dog's food from one type to another do so gradually, mixing small amounts of the new food into the meals until the change-over is slowly completed.

The adult weight of a female Entlebucher is around 22-24kg and therefore they fall into the medium sized dog category. Males tend to be around 27-28kg and are therefore classed as large for the sake of feeding. The only real difference in the food seems to be the size of the pieces and as dry food can provide a good source of teeth cleaning this is important. If the pieces are too small for the dog, he will swallow them rather than chew. Please note, the weights mentioned will vary if your dog is a smaller, or larger build. A bitch may be as small as 20kg and a dog as much as 30kg without being under or overweight. Comparing with other owners is only applicable if you have dogs of a similar height to the shoulder and similar build, otherwise it is best to judge on an individual basis and bear in mind they should be well muscled rather than slight in stature, but nicely in proportion overall.

Wheat intolerance is not uncommon. If you have a dog that has issues of loose stools, wind and occasional sickness, you might want to experiment with a wheat free food to see if that makes a difference. Remember to check any treats being given as well as the dog's main food. There can be many other causes of the symptoms described, so a vet should be consulted if you are concerned. A healthy dog on a good diet should have well-formed stools that are easy to clean up. Incorrect feeding early in the puppy's life can lead to stunted growth, bad teeth and poor bone formation in the adult dog.

Poisons

A dog will not always make wise choices about food left in an accessible place

Some human food can be toxic to dogs even in small amounts. It is easy to assume that foods which humans can eat will also be safe for your dog. However, many foods we eat contain toxins and even different humans may be more or less capable to tolerate those toxins. For some humans a very low level of toxin may cause them to be ill. The same is true of dogs.

There are foods, commonly tolerated by humans, which even in very small quantities may prove dangerous or even fatal to a dog. You will regularly hear people say that their dog has eaten something and was fine, but NEVER take that to mean that your dog will be fine too. It is not just about a toxin causing an upset stomach, in some instances even a tiny amount can cause catastrophic organ failure in a dog.

Listed below are food stuffs which are potentially very dangerous to a dog and should NEVER be given as part of their diet. Whilst that might sound like me being a killjoy, there are plenty of alternatives that dogs can have which are specifically designed for their needs.

If you do insist on giving them human foodstuffs then read the ingredient list on the packet to be on the safe side – an example of this would be gravy – which normally contains onion if it is made from granules or powder and onion is toxic to dogs. Also remember, something which has been cooked including any of these ingredients is as unsafe as the item on its own.

This is one area where loving your dog means respecting that he or she is a dog and is not just a small human. It also means realising that just because he wants it, does not mean it's good for him!

This list is not exhaustive, but these are items that are potentially toxic to dogs:

Apple (seeds – contain cyanide)
Apricot
Avocado
Chives
Chocolate
Currants and raisins
Dough (uncooked)
Garlic
Grapes
Hops
Macadamia nuts
Onions
Palm oil
Potato (green)
Rhubarb (leaves)
Star Fruit
Sultanas
Walnut
Xylitol - a common constituent of yoghurt, amongst other products

Also note the following plants are highly poisonous to dogs

Azaleas and Rhododendrons
Tulip and Daffodil Bulbs

Tulip and daffodil bulbs are poisonous to dogs

Many types of mushroom
Beech trees
Foxgloves
Laburnum
Sago palms
Nightshade
Peony
Snow drops
Yew
Yucca

Exercise

In the early life of a puppy it is essential that as little stress is put on the joints as possible. Try to prevent him using stairs or steps for as long as possible and do not do any agility training, where jumping is involved, until the joints are fully developed. Of course, with an Entlebucher saying 'no jumping' is not always

Torfheide Chekov (Otto)

understood by the dog and in the early months / years they can seem to be on springs.

In terms of exercise, the normal rule of thumb is no more than five minutes per month of life. At three months that would mean walks of no longer than a quarter of an hour of continuous movement and so on. If it is a slow gentle stroll with plenty of rests then longer than this will not be so much of a problem. However, particularly if they are running around it is wise to be relatively strict to prevent joint damage occurring.

The amount of exercise they will need when they are older will vary from dog to dog and between breeding lines. Some will be happy with a good brisk half an hour walk each day, and other more gentle exercise in between. Others will need substantially longer. It is important to bear in mind that in general they will be able to go all day if required, as that was what would have been needed in a working capacity. However, do consider this may be affected by how fit you keep your dog.

You will also find as a puppy, and often well into later life, an Entlebucher will get the 'zoomies' and, for no apparent reason that you can see as a human, will spend ten minutes running laps as though his life depends on it. They will do this whether they are in the lounge or the garden. He will stop just as suddenly as he started and act as though nothing odd just happened. This is normal, annoying at times, entertaining at others, but definitely normal.

Grooming

Entlebuchers require only maintenance grooming, perhaps every month or two, although this can be done more frequently if desired. To remove dead hair when moulting, and at other times to make them look their best, it is good to use a grooming mitt. This is an enjoyable experience for both the dog and his owner. Always brush in the direction of the fur and never against it, being particularly careful around any sensitive areas.

Entlebuchers moult seasonally in spring and autumn for dogs and about four to eight weeks prior to their seasons for bitches.

Your dog will, given the opportunity, keep himself meticulously clean. After a muddy walk, a wipe down with ordinary warm water should be enough. The dogs will then groom themselves. Bathing your dog is rarely required. When you feel it necessary then use a gentle baby shampoo or specially formulated dog shampoo, or just warm water. Shampoo should not be used regularly as it breaks down the natural protective oils in the coat.

Torfheide Cuddles (Scout)

Listening to your dog

An Entlebucher will talk to his owner. He may not use words and phrases, but don't underestimate the range of noises he will use and different expressions he has to convey meaning. If you take the time to listen to your dog and observe him closely it will not take long for you to tune into his conversation.

The most common communication an owner will understand is when the dog wants a particular part of his body rubbed. He will make this very clear by directing your hand to the particular spot he has in mind and whilst this is commonly the chest, there are other times it will be his back or head.

If one of his legs is hurting he will commonly lick at the paw of that leg. It does not necessarily mean the discomfort is coming from the paw itself. In some instances, if he has a health problem he will bring it to you and present you with the offending part.

With my own dogs, the eldest will always be the one to come to tell me if one of the others needs the toilet and I have not realised. To do that he will bark at me until I respond to find out what the problem is.

If their behaviour seems odd, instead of dismissing it or being annoyed, try to put yourself in their mindset

Never underestimate how loud an Entlebucher can bark!

and see if you can work out what is on their mind. Sometimes it will be as basic as wanting food or to go to the toilet, but other times they may be needing some reassurance and a gentle word. They may have four legs and fur, but in many ways they are similar to humans.

Training

Entlebuchers are very bright dogs. They are also the best trainers in the world! They know what they want and they know how to get it! In an ideal world, they need training before they train their owners, although in reality it will be a two-way process. This is not intended as a complete training guide for your dog and there is no substitute for finding good classes for you and your dog to attend on an ongoing basis. Classes will give him socialisation skills as well as training and are invaluable.

Wilma v. Rickental with her Good Citizen Bronze certificate

Keep in mind that what your dog learns will not just come from the commands you use when formally training him. Everything you do will be noted and patterns understood. You should therefore be consistent at all times and see everyday interactions as training opportunities. This also keeps it fun. An Entlebucher will pick up on things you do or say regularly even when you don't recognise your own habits. In an everyday situation this may be as simple as finding there is a trigger word you use when you are about to get up and be active. I had the habit of saying 'Right' as I went to get up. The dogs realised this even if I didn't and the use of that word meant they were ready to go.

In training classes it is quite common to be taught when doing heel work to lead off with your left foot, but to lead off with the right if you are doing an exercise where the dog is not to move immediately, a 'wait' or a 'stay'. With a bright dog who reads your body movements this will also mean you can drop the commands and they will still know what you have in mind… as long as you are consistent!

Taking your Entlebucher to a training class can be very hard work if you don't find the right classes. Your dog is bright. Of course, there are other breeds which are intelligent, but an Entlebucher is a match for almost any. If you find yourself in a class of dogs who take much longer to understand what is required when your dog has understood the exercise first time, then you can find yourself with a lot of waiting around and a very bored Entlebucher. Make sure you are fully prepared with games and mini-exercises to keep him entertained until such a point as you have developed a patient 'stay' which can be used for an extended period of time. The alternative is that they bark… and bark… demanding attention and wanting to know what the next activity is.

It can work well for their training to be combined with a high energy activity such as agility, where they are learning to focus on you very closely, but also use more physical energy than in standard obedience classes.

Our first puppy classes were in a waterlogged field, at night, and in Flemish, a language I was not familiar with. The classes did not go well for us. By the time we understood what we were supposed to be doing, the others in the class had moved on to the next exercise. My dog wasn't enjoying them. I wasn't enjoying them and it wasn't the best learning environment as a result.

An Entlebucher will love to learn tricks. This can be a good way to keep him occupied, although if you are using training treats then use the food from his meal and cut his mealtime food so you don't end up over-feeding him.

I did start trying to teach one of my dogs, Aristotle, to read commands from cards. However, it takes a lot of time and patience as they learn to recognise the shape of the word as you say them. It's a good party trick if you can do it and they are more than capable - on the whole the thing that holds them back is the amount of time we are prepared to devote to their training. Many times around the house they will simply learn how things work by observation, even without instruction. That can be good or bad depending on what they pick up. When visiting a friend who had kitchen cupboard doors which opened when gently pressed, Aristotle accidentally opened one cupboard door. He then started deliberately opening other doors to see if there was anything interesting. I do find the overarching commands of 'Leave It' and 'No' can be very useful!

These are the very basic commands it is worth every dog learning:

'Leave' or 'Leave it' – given when you want him not to pick something up, or if he has picked it up to put it down immediately. This is not a command he would be released from. What I mean by that is, you would not use it for a biscuit that you are going to allow him to have at some point in the future. It is an absolute not now not ever. It is useful for everything from him going to take something in the home that is not his, to chasing the neighbour's cat, to picking up a dead animal when out walking.

Practising 'Wait'

'No' – a quick command to stop him doing an action you don't want him to do. If the thing he is doing is chewing on something that is inappropriate because he is teething and his gums are sore, please remember he is like a baby and needs something else to chew on instead and should not just be left to feel uncomfortable.

'Wait' – this is a command from which he will be released. You don't want him to do something 'yet' – so that might be you ask him to 'sit' and 'wait' until he is called to 'come' to you, or it may be to make him 'wait' before taking his food when you tell him it is 'ok'.

48

'Ok' – a simple command to reassure the dog he is allowed to do something or to release him from a holding command. An Entlebucher will look to you for direction. It is easy to give a reassuring 'ok' with a nod of the head, so that you can permit something with or without words.

'Sit' – used to get your dog to sit down. It is easiest to train a command by using the word when he is actually doing the action you want to achieve, then praise him for it. If you say the word as he does the action, then very soon he will make the connection. After a while when you say the command he will know that is what is associated with the word. You can also use a treat in your hand and when the dog is facing you take your hand with the treat over his head as you say the word 'sit'. He will most likely move backwards into a sit position to bring his nose level with the treat. Praise your dog and give him the treat.

'Go' – I use this as the basic toilet command. I find it an unembarrassing term to use when parked at a service station or shouted out of the back door morning, night etc. As with 'sit' use it when he does go to the toilet in the right place as a puppy, so that he begins to associate the word with the action and reward accordingly.

Attempting a group stay - UK Southern Fun Day 2016

'Stay' – this is distinct from 'wait' as you plan to return to your dog rather than him coming to you.

'**Lie down**' – when I want him to lie as distinct from 'down' when I don't want him to jump up.

'**Bed**' – when I want him to find somewhere comfortable to lie down out of the way, often accompanied by me pointing to where I want him to go. It can also be useful to teach him

Lie Down

'crate' when you specifically want him to go to his crate.

'**Come**' – when I want a dog to come to me.

'**Heel**' – when I want him to walk, without pulling, by my left heel. If you want him to walk to the right it is worth having a different command for this so you can quickly call him to the position you want, such as when there is oncoming traffic and you are walking on a country lane.

Another common one I use is '**Hup**' to tell him when I am inviting him to put his paws up on me, as opposed to '**Down**' when he has done that to me or someone else uninvited.

There are also basic commands worth teaching your dog to make health examinations easy. I have included these in the introduction to the health section.

Socialisation

Socialisation of a dog is extremely important to ensure your pet enjoys a happy and balanced life. From the very start, a breeder should begin to expose a puppy to a wide variety of experiences within the confines of a safe environment. This should be continued by the new owner when the puppy goes to his home. In doing this there are a number of things to remember. As a dog goes through his major growth phases he will need rest periods as well as periods of activity. Constant new experiences will be too much for him and they should be interspersed with times to relax. Whatever he encounters while young and is made to feel comfortable with, will stand him in good stead for his life to come. This needs to cover everything from bicycles to wheelchairs, beards to turbans, toddlers to the elderly. His socialisation should also include traffic, crowds and other animals as well as plenty of opportunity to socialise amongst other dogs and learn manners in playing with and around them.

Thought should be given to all the puppy's senses, with situations of different noises, touch, sights and for that matter smells. To acclimatise a puppy to noises there are some very good sound tracks that can be bought with everything from thunder, to children playing, to low flying planes. Playing these sounds to the puppy when they are relaxed and settled can help the puppy understand that such noises are nothing they need to be concerned about.

If experiences are missed during socialisation some very odd situations can arise at a later date. Even rucksacks or long camera lenses can be off-putting if they are not introduced until later in life.

During this socialisation, thought needs to be given to a puppy's fear stages. I've mentioned these under the different age sections. Anything which causes trauma in these stages can stay with the puppy as a fear throughout his life and may cause problems.

As this is regularly when a puppy transfers to his new home it is important that every measure is taken for these changes to be effected with as little stress as possible. This is where

A puppy rucksack makes it possible to take a pup out ahead of his vaccinations

the 'comforter' mentioned in 'Taking Your Puppy Home' can be highly effective. It helps the puppy to feel as though he 'knows' his family long before the move takes place.

A second fear stage takes place from around six months of age and can last until the puppy is around fourteen months old. It is important to be mindful of situations during this period which could lead to a problem. There can also be a change in reactions through the teenage phase as the hormones become fully operational. At this stage the dog feels greater independence and may begin to instinctively show guarding tendencies.

Emergency Arrangements

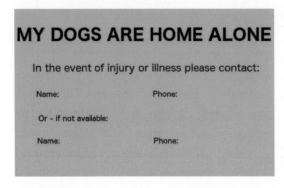

MY DOGS ARE HOME ALONE

In the event of injury or illness please contact:

Name: Phone:

Or - if not available:

Name: Phone:

Your responsibility to your dogs means having emergency arrangements in place. These are not just for the very worst case scenario, but to cover everyday eventualities which can and do occur. If you are taken ill, delayed somewhere, even stuck in a prolonged traffic jam or your car breaks down, what are your arrangements for your dog(s)? This should be covered in advance of the problem occurring. Does someone have a key to your home? Can someone feed and take your dogs out, or if necessary collect them and take them somewhere they can be looked after?

In some circumstances, where you may not be in a position to contact someone easily, it is worth carrying a card in your wallet or other location where it will be found easily, giving details for emergency contact. 'My dog(s) are home alone. Please contact…'

Your arrangements should also include what will happen to your dogs if you should die. Whilst it is not a situation anyone wants to think about, you do need to consider what is in the best interests of your dog. If you do not have anyone in your circle of friends or family who would provide continued care for your dog, then make sure the dog's breeder and / or the Entlebucher Club Rescue contact is listed for that eventuality.

Children and Dogs

There is something wonderful about watching a young child and puppy growing up together. An Entlebucher is by nature especially gentle with children and can be the perfect companion. However, no matter how good your think your dog is, a young child should always be supervised when with the dog. For one thing, the child needs to learn what are and what are not acceptable behaviours. It can seem a fun game to a child to sit astride the dog, pull his ears or tail, poke him or any one of a number of other unacceptable situations. A dog can only be expected to take so much. Within the pack if a fellow pack member continues to annoy, then a quick nip in response is perfectly reasonable dog behaviour to dissuade the guilty

There is no more beautiful relationship than an Entlebucher growing up with a young child

party. You do not want your dog to resort to nipping a provoking child. Part of this is teaching the dog tolerance, but the major part is teaching the child respect.

I've already explained that the dog's pattern of behaviour for his adult life is shaped while he is young. Allowing family members (old or young) to play roughly with a puppy sets the pattern of behaviour that the dog will think acceptable at a later date.

An owner should also be aware of legislation in their own country. Some places specify a minimum age at which a child can be in control of a dog without adult supervision. Certainly, given the strength of an Entlebucher, it is also wise to think about whether a child has the strength to control the dog if a problem occurs.

Using Their Intelligence

This is an intelligent breed and it helps if you realise just how intelligent they are. They will of course copy things that they see done, but also work some things out for themselves. At six months old, having watched one of the others lose a chew under a chair cushion, Aristotle waited for the other dog to get down. He then went and removed the cushion and found the chew, but he did not stop there. He put the cushion back on the chair before climbing up to sit in comfort and enjoy his prize. He is also the dog who can stand at a kitchen work surface and use his front legs as arms to hold a closed container and his nose to take the lid off, so he can get to the contents.

An owner of an Entlebucher needs to think ahead and look at the world through their dog's eyes to see what mischief they might get up to given the opportunity. They also need to ensure that anything potentially harmful to their dogs is kept locked away... and the key not left accessible!

The best thing to do is to channel your dog's abilities so that he uses them constructively. He can be trained to do a very wide variety of tricks and tasks if an owner puts the time in to training him.

Escaping From Crates

Many owners think that crating a dog when he is left unattended will be the perfect and easy solution and it is to a point. I used to think that crates were dreadful and that I would never want to use one. However, once I learned that my dogs love having a crate as a safe place they can take their prizes to, away from the others, or go to for a quiet sleep if they want to get away from it all, I changed my view. A crate needs to give a full-grown dog plenty of space to stretch out and stand up and turn around, but it can be a very useful addition to the household. However, be warned it took one of my dogs exactly five minutes to work out how to dismantle the side of her crate to get out. My first thought was that this was a simple stroke of luck so I put it to the test. I put a camera on the crate and ensured the crate was firmly and correctly set up. I timed Wilma as she used her paws as hands, holding the side as she pulled it first one way and then the other to disconnect the panel - three minutes! This time she knew exactly what she had to do.

From experience securing the sides with cable ties is pointless as they can be chewed through too easily, the thick grey duct tape is the best solution, but even that will need replacing at intervals.

Toys and Games

There are some very good 'brain games' that you can buy for your Entlebucher, however do not be surprised when the gets the hang of them in a matter of minutes. Whether he has to remove pieces to find the treat or push blocks aside to access other blocks, it will not take long, but it will be fun and makes a great party trick. Where possible, buy games that are marked as being the most difficult level as these will take marginally longer to complete.

Aristotle with some of his games

In general the best I am aware of are the Nina Ottoson range of advanced puzzles http://www.nina-ottosson.com/ or Trixie strategy games https://www.trixie.de/heimtierbedarf/us/shop/Dog/ActivityGames/. I have one by Trixie where the pad to activate the treat can be placed in a different room to the treat dispenser making the dog have to go to find it each time.

COMMON ISSUES

There are a number of subjects which come up repeatedly as topics which give owners concern when bringing up an Entlebucher. Most can be addressed fairly easily, but all will require gentle firmness and total consistency in approach. Basically, an Entlebucher wants to please his human. However, if you are not positively reinforcing the good behaviours and giving him the right amount of attention, he will take the approach that any attention is better than none and will use whatever behaviours he needs to get you to react. If you turn to the technique of using training exercises or practising tricks as a way to get him to refocus when misbehaving, it can at times be counterproductive. If what he wanted was your attention this may mean he has won and his bad behaviour has succeeded in getting what he wanted. This rapidly becomes a vicious circle. Giving him a time out and returning to him when he is quiet and behaving well takes more effort, but will teach the dog that good behaviour rather than bad is what will be rewarded with your attention.

Bite Inhibition

Dogs getting 'mouthy' and biting can be a big problem if it happens, however doing a few things from a young age should mean the problem can be avoided.

There are two parts to dealing with this. One is to ensure when they use their mouths they do so gently and the other is to ensure when they do need to chew, they do not do so on the wrong things.

Never encourage rough

Dogs use their mouths in play – Wilma with Torfheide D'Artagnan (Leo)

play with a puppy. It may seem fun, but a puppy whose human laughs when the puppy bites and nips at human hands will think it is acceptable behaviour. The growing dog will not understand why a behaviour that has been all right before, suddenly becomes unacceptable as he grows. For the human, what might have seemed a game will become a problem. If a puppy instigates rough play, as he would with his litter mates, then as his teeth come into contact with flesh the human should yelp, making a noise to indicate pain even if none has actually been caused. When the puppy stops then praise the puppy. Done consistently this should encourage him only to use his mouth softly and without teeth. As he starts to do well you can take this a step further by deliberately putting your hand or arm in his mouth and praising him when he does not react.

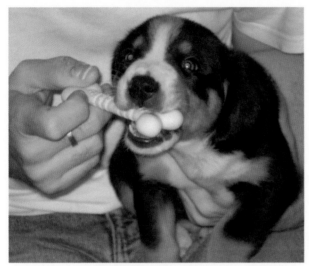

Torfheide Alan (Rafa)

If a puppy needs to chew, always have something appropriate handy. A puppy does need chew toys. Like a human baby he will go through stages of teething. His first teeth come through from around week four onwards, much to the discomfort of the mother. These milk teeth will begin to fall out at around three or four months. Over the next few months the adult teeth will start to come through and the dog will have a major need to chew as this happens. Have something like a teething ring, a chew toy, or dog chew that he can bite on at those times. Then if he reaches for your arm, hand, tv remote etc. immediately substitute his chew toy. When you do this on a repeated basis he quickly gets the message and picks up the right item.

Puppies and even adult dogs can become 'bitey' when they are overexcited or overtired. If that is, or even might be, the case, move him into a quiet environment where he can calm down or sleep as appropriate. If you are away from the house and it is an adult dog that is the issue, then insist on the dog lying down and then verbally hold him in a stay for long enough for him to calm down. You might even gently massage the dog's shoulders to speed up the relaxation process. Another approach with an overexcited dog is simply to hold him close to you for a few minutes until he is calm.

Also remember he is a herding dog and he would use a 'nip' to get a cow to go in the direction he wants them to go in. If you find yourself being the cow then remember he is forgetting that he takes instruction from you and not the other way around. Give him a time out without your attention, be strict with him in a 'stay' while he is lying down or another command in which he is focussed on you being in charge, but for which he is not being rewarded and is not having fun. Once he has calmed down, release him from the command but continue to give him instructions while you stay in charge, such as walking to heel, maintaining eye contact, or doing a few training exercises until he is completely working with you again.

Barking

One characteristic of the Entlebucher is his voice. He is not by habit a noisy dog, and around the house can be extremely quiet, particularly if not kept with other dogs. However, given the opportunity to express himself, he can turn out an impressive vocal range that can sound more like conversation than simply a barking dog.

Once you bear in mind that their voices have to be heard across mountain valleys, you will realise that, when they do bark, it can be VERY loud. This can be difficult, with problems ranging from making you jump when you are least expecting it to finding yourself ejected from a training class until your dog will be quiet. For some reason, even a normally quiet Entlebucher seems to think that a training class is the perfect time to exercise his vocal cords and very few of the tips that trainers provide seem to work. Keeping the dog totally focussed and working is the most effective. Of course, this means devising working exercises in between your dog's turn to take part in class exercises and holding his attention at all times. There is more on this in the section on training.

Wilma demanding attention

One thing to be careful about when correcting a barking issue is that barking is a way of gaining attention. If you then start to do other exercises or play with the dog to keep him quiet, then in his terms he has achieved what he set out to do and his barking has worked. In deciding how to deal with the barking the first step is to identify the cause.

1) Barking to alert you to some event - in this situation the dog may be telling you there is something he genuinely thinks you need to know. This may be someone at the door, or in the case of one of my dogs the fact that one of the others needs to go out! If that is the reason then thank your dog, reward him for a correct behaviour and deal with what it is he has told you. Quiet should be restored.

2) Barking through over-excitement - the responses to this are similar to bite inhibition. Take an action to calm your dog. Either put him into a stay in the down position and expect him to remain in place until the excitement has passed, put him in another room or put him in his crate for a time out, until he has calmed, or hold him in a firm embrace until he is once more relaxed and happy.

3) Barking in play - Entlebuchers commonly make a lot of noise when playing with other dogs. Unfortunately, whilst these noises do not represent an issue which needs to be dealt with, many other pet owners are concerned by the barking and think there is a problem with your dog. Most of the time, there is no problem at all except that an Entlebucher often uses his voice when playing.

4) Barking due to uncertainty - a dog that is unsure of his ground is liable to bark. One important thing is to have

Alfie with Cara-Isabella v. Kornried (Izzy)

socialised the puppy as thoroughly as possible while he is young, but also to continue to expose him to a wide variety of situations until he is fully mature. Don't push your dog if he is uncomfortable with a situation as that may reinforce his concern. However, do show him that you are comfortable. If his human is confident and unconcerned then the bond these dogs have with us means that very often they will be happy that if it is good enough for you then it's good enough for him. Having said that, I'm tempted to say 'they are only human', at least in as much as there are situations which some dogs do not cope with, for example as mentioned earlier, confined spaces. Look ahead for situations which may cause a problem and try to find an alternative approach.

5) Barking on meeting strangers - see the section on wariness and protection.

6) Barking due to confusion in old age - Alfie has canine cognitive dysfunction (dog dementia). He barks when he is confused. I know absolutely no solution to this problem other than providing a safe well-known environment, lots of love and patience and a set of ear-plugs - for you rather than the dog!

Another approach which can be taken with barking is to teach your dog to bark on command. In doing so, you also teach a 'finish' command to stop him barking. When he then barks at times that are not appropriate the 'finish' command can be used to silence him as though the original barking had been under instruction. Sadly, I have never achieved this with our dogs. I suspect it is rather easier if you are dealing with training one dog than multiple dogs who then react to each other's barking!

None of the above covers aggressive behaviour. If your dog exhibits aggressive behaviour then it is time to call in expert help.

Ball Obsession

It is almost always fun to play ball with your dog. Having said that, one of my dogs does not understand playing ball however hard both I and my other dogs try to teach her, but she is a rare example. Entlebuchers generally love playing ball, so much so that the biggest risk is that once he has started he does not want to stop. The second risk is that he gets so excited that when you reach for the ball, he goes for your hand in his excitement, resulting in pain to you.

Play ball in short bursts and make sure that amongst the commands you teach

Alfie with his talking ball

him are 'drop' so he puts the ball down, 'wait' so he doesn't pick it up again if you are not ready and 'finish' or 'game over' when play has come to an end. It also makes sense to ask your dog to sit nicely and wait while you retrieve the ball ready to throw again, so that you are not both going to pick it up at the same time. If your dog becomes fixated on playing ball, that is not a healthy reaction and it is wise to stop playing altogether. Problems may also come when he has played too long and is overtired. Sometimes these dogs just don't know when to stop.

If you want to keep your dog playing long after you have got bored, then there are automatic ball throwers that you can buy to launch the ball, which rely on you teaching the dog to bring the ball back and put it into the slot for the ball to be launched again… and again… and again!

If you have a dog who likes playing ball nicely, but does not always remember to bring the ball back neatly to your feet or hand, then it is worth buying old tennis balls in bulk from a tennis club that has finished with them, when they move on to new balls. However, if you are using tennis balls also be aware that the nylon of the ball does wear the dog's teeth down over time and a regular ball playing dog will end up with significant tooth damage.

Herding

Herding is natural and instinctive to an Entlebucher. This can have cute moments when he rounds up all his toys and makes sure they are in one place, and it can have very annoying moments, when he tries to round up the family when out for a walk. It is more natural to an Entlebucher to circle you and keep you together than it is to walk to heel. This can be entertaining when due to family argument you try to walk some distance apart. Your dog will dart back and forth desperately trying to round you back up.

Do not underestimate the Entlebucher's fascination with cows

Equally, if for any reason one of your party has to leave the group it will take the dog a while to accept that he should not be bringing them back. These behaviours can be fun or annoying depending on how you see them. However, around livestock it is very important that an untrained herding dog is kept firmly on the lead and not left to try his own amateur sheepdog trials, otherwise you face the risk of farmers with shotguns taking actions which could be catastrophic. If you have the opportunity to put your dog through some training with livestock, then do it. Although my dogs have not had the chance, from those I have seen who have, they will love the opportunity.

It is always interesting to observe an Entlebucher's reaction around cows. It is quite different from when they are around any other animals. Somehow they know. Imprinted on their genes is an understanding of the basics that this is what they were born for. Nature is amazing.

Wariness and Protection

Part of the role that the dogs undertake in their normal working environment is protection of the farm. They do have some natural guarding behaviours as I have already explained. They are also by nature wary of strangers, until they decide someone is a part of their pack and therefore to be trusted and welcomed. This can take them from a matter of minutes to significantly longer depending on their experiences and the dog in question's individual character and for that matter the character of the person they are deciding whether to welcome. Even a well socialised dog, who as a puppy seems to welcome one and all, will from the age of around eighteen months start to show some of these characteristics.

A dog barking in their face can be off-putting to many strangers and many people do feel threatened by it. Reassurance by the owner that there is nothing to be concerned about does not satisfy everyone. When you are out, keeping your dog close to you and under control is important. Although I'm more likely to find Wilma with her nose in someone's picnic hamper, Shadow may make her presence felt in a very loud fashion.

Defence Training - Photo Daniela Ranglová - Czech Republic

Their guarding instinct can extend to when you are out walking. If you are a lone female walking a dog and meet an unknown man, be prepared for your dog to react. However, if you start to be concerned that they will react then you will tighten the lead and pass your concern down the lead to the dog, thus reinforcing their worry that there is something they should react to. Being as relaxed as possible but having control over your dog is the best approach you can take.

There is a big difference between barking and growling. If a dog is in a situation they are not comfortable with then they will show this by their body language and their voice. If a dog growls at you or your dog growls at someone else, that is definitely not the time to approach that dog thinking you know better. The dog is asking you to back off and that is exactly what you should do. Pushing your hand in front of the dog's face at this point, when they already feel threatened, and you thinking all will be well if the dog smells you, is simply asking for your hand to be bitten.

If your dog barks at someone, the dog is making his presence known and saying who is boss. If he growls at someone then listen to your dog and take the dog out of the situation. Otherwise there is the potential for things not to end well!

Jumping

If I had £1 for every owner who has asked me how to stop their dog jumping up… well I'd have almost as many pounds as there are UK dogs. Entlebuchers jump. They can jump several feet in the air from a standing start and suddenly kiss you on the lips. They can also run at you at full pelt in greeting and come close to knocking you over. They can be stopped from jumping, but it takes patience and consistency. Refusing to greet them until they have all four paws on the floor, or better still are sitting nicely in front of you can be a very good behaviour to teach them from a young age. Another tip to prevent them reaching their target, is to gently raise your knee as you see them approach so that they cannot get close to your body. Of course that can leave you on one leg when they finally run into you, which can in itself have unfortunate consequences.

What will not work is to tell them off for doing it one minute and then encourage them to do it the next. In this respect, all members of the household need to be consistent.

Wilma jumping

I teach my dogs a command to invite them to stand up on their hind legs and put their front paws on me. When they get that command they can do it with permission. If they do not receive that command then such behaviour will not be welcomed. One of my dogs, Aristotle, is so proficient at walking on two legs that it is not so much jumping up as wrapping his front legs around me and he does it so gently that he is always likely to make me smile.

Their ability to jump has also left me watching one of them clearing the sofa from back to front in a game of chase with another dog around the lounge. In the case of Wilma it means she sees any sort of a dog gate as simply something to practise hurdling and not a barrier to free movement.

Separation

Entlebuchers like human company above all else. They bond very closely with their prime carer and, even with other company around, will miss their designated human. It is particularly important to accustom an Entlebucher to time on his own and this takes specific thought and training. Ensuring there is time apart when your dog is a puppy is an important first step. Initially this should be for very short periods, but should be built up over time.

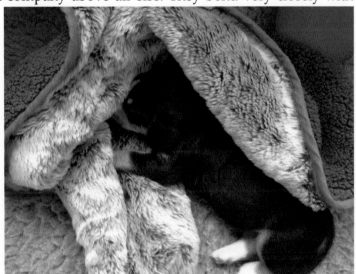

Torfheide Casanova (Otis) having his first time apart from the rest of the litter

Whilst the puppy is on his own he should be left with toys and challenges to keep him occupied and it is best to have exercised him first. One of the most effective 'games' can be a frozen Kong toy or previously filled bone re-stuffed with a combination of kibble, yoghurt, banana etc. and then frozen. If you know in advance that the dog needs to be left, it can be good to give them their meal in this form so that they have to spend a good length of time working to gain their food. This in itself will prove satisfying. As mentioned earlier, it is also very useful to do this when a puppy is teething.

Torfheide Beethoven (Basil) getting used to time alone

If you have to leave your dog for more than a few hours then he should have someone go in to him part way through, to allow the dog a toilet break and a chance to stretch his legs.

Even if you rarely have need to leave your dog for more than a few minutes at a time, it is wise to train him to be comfortable in his own company, so that if the need arises it is not a problem. It is never possible to predict when something may occur that necessitates time away from our loved ones. An Entlebucher will pine for his human unless he feels safe and confident that his human will return and that all will be well.

For the same reasons, if you plan to go away without your dog, think ahead to what your arrangements will be. Whether you are planning to use a pet-sitter, have your dog stay with family or friends, or use a good kennels then acclimatise him to this from a young age. In order for your dog to be confident that you will always come back, start him with a short daytime occasion when you leave him. Build that up to an overnight stay, then a weekend, before leaving him for any longer period. As long as your dog is confident that you will always return to him, then he is likely to settle and have a happy stay. Always leave him with something that smells of you in the early visits, to make sure he can take comfort from having your scent around.

When you greet your Entlebucher having not seen him for a while, those are the times that you are most likely to find that jumping becomes a problem and many bruises can be gained. If you can be disciplined with yourself, rather than give in to your own overwhelming pleasure at seeing your dog, then is the time to make him sit quietly in order to be greeted. Even a puppy can chip one of your teeth in an excited and uncontrolled greeting - I have the evidence to prove it!

DOG SPORTS

Entlebuchers can be very athletic and work hard at any task that is asked of them. However, bearing in mind their tendency to throw themselves into activities and what has been written later in the book about cruciate ligament tears, some degree of caution should be taken when considering involving your dog in sport. Always use an experienced and proficient trainer who will be able to guide you and your dog safely through the learning. Don't push your dog too far or start when they are too young. Do give your dog full opportunity to recover from any injury before doing any further sport. I can also highly recommend swimming as a way for your dog to build his muscles without putting a strain on his frame. However, even swimming can have its risks and dogs can strain the muscles in the tail as they use them to give balance and direction. No one wants a dog not to be able to wag his tail while he is recovering!

Carting

Our breed has pulled carts as part of their working life. They love to work and pulling a cart is something they enjoy given the opportunity. It is very important that they only ever pull a cart which is designed for their shape and size and that the weight they pull is appropriate. It is also vital that they have the right equipment

Norfolkfields Benji (Eiger) with training wheels (Photo Lizz Alexander)

and training. It is not simply a question of attaching a cart and away they go!

The initial step is for a dog to become accustomed to wearing a harness. From there the dog needs to get used to pulling something behind him without trying to get away from it. When the UK Club organised a carting training session, the dogs started with a milk carton, followed by a small log. After that, to get more of an idea of pulling a weight, they progressed to a larger log, before finally moving on to an open frame with training wheels. This is all necessary to get the dog used to both the sensations involved and being prepared to walk in a straight line with something behind him.

Wilma carrying her own things for Crufts

On a smaller scale, investing in a small dog rucksack and making your dog carry his own things when you go for a walk can be a rewarding experience for both dog and owner. It is very interesting to see the difference in the dogs when they go into 'working' mode, which mine tend to do, the moment their rucksack is fitted. You will need to allow extra time anywhere you go however, not for the load slowing progress, but for complete strangers wanting to take your dog's photograph.

Agility

'Agility' is a dog sport that plays to the strengths particularly of female Entlebuchers. They are fast, agile and love to work. Whether going through weaving poles, over jumps or through tunnels, an Entlebucher will have a lot of fun over an agility course. However, no jumping should be encouraged until the dog's joints are fully formed. I realise this may seem a crazy statement, when around the house the dog is leaping and jumping with almost every step, but the less any additional pressure is applied to developing joints the better it will be for the dog, particularly in later life.

Males often fare slightly less well through things such as the weaving poles, with the length of their body being less conducive to fast twists and turns in that way. However, it depends on the build of the dog and a slightly smaller, slimmer built dog may do just as well as a bitch.

It is a fun activity for both dog and owner and is a good way of burning off excess energy while using the dog's brain at the same time.

Photo Jirka Wasserbauer - Czech Republic

Flyball

Flyball is a fast, high-energy sport that combines several activities an Entlebucher loves. It is a team relay race in which two dogs run in neighbouring lanes over a number of hurdles, before pressing a pedal to release a ball that he brings back on his homeward leg, before the next dog takes over. The winner of the heat is the team whose four dogs complete the exercise in relay and cross the winning line first. Where it is within a competition, the two teams will run either three or five repeats of the course to determine the overall winner who will then go through to the next round.

It is a high impact sport, so again I would caution with regards to both the risk of injury to the dog and the age at which he begins. However, there can't be many Entlebuchers who would not enjoy the combination of speed, jumping and a ball to bring back!

Rally or Rally-O

Rally is a derivation of obedience work. It involves dogs and handlers competing over different exercises as they move around the course area. The instructions are all given by written signs at those points of the course where they must take place, rather than verbal commands from a judge. There are different levels that a dog can attain and reaching a higher level is based on a series of separately judged assessments. In the early levels the dog works on lead, but the highest levels require off-lead working. The exercises differ slightly from standard competitive obedience and some, such as the group stay, are not included.

Treibball or Drive Ball

Treibball is probably the best sport for an Entlebucher, although sadly it is not yet widely available in the UK. It was devised in Germany and is a game that uses the

Photo Bohdana Stoklasova Czech Republic

dog's herding ability, but without the need for livestock. It involves moving eight large exercise-size balls from a triangular starting point, like a snooker ball set-up, to a pen the size of a football goal. The balls must stay within the bounds of the playing area and the handler gives instruction to the dog on which ball to move and where they need to go.

There is a time limit and restrictions on how far from the goal the handler can move. Also, the dog must not bite the ball. Essentially the bond between handler and dog is much the same as required to move livestock and the handler must work with whistles, shouts and hand signals to get the dog to go around the balls and drive them one by one into the goal. This is by far the closest sport to the natural abilities of our breed and unlike some other dog sports is more about using intelligence and speed, than it is about high impact activities.

OPPORTUNITIES TO WORK

There are still some of the breed working in their original herding capacity, but these are fairly rare. However, an Entlebucher is capable of working in other spheres as well as making a remarkable family pet.

Search and Rescue

Photo Hana Vaculinova, Czech Republic

There are Entlebuchers who are being trained in search and rescue in a number of countries. As can be seen in the photograph, dogs are training in Search and Rescue in the Czech Republic, mostly in the field of 'rubble search'. In the UK there are dogs learning lowland work with the South East London Search and Rescue organisation (SELSAR). Qualification is incredibly difficult and needs a considerable time commitment from both dog and handler.

In Switzerland there are dogs who have completed their mountain rescue training and keep their skills up to date.

Therapy Dogs

Many Entlebuchers can make good therapy dogs. In order for them to work in this way, their owner will need to help them overcome any uncertainty with strangers and not all Entlebuchers would be suitable. Most are naturally good around children and as a breed their nature makes them well suited to therapy work with younger people. They would be very well suited to school reading projects for reluctant readers.

To pass their character test for working as a therapy dog, an owner will have needed to address any issue of them jumping up of course!

Special Detection Work

For a number of years, Isone Uit't Holandse Entlinest has, with her owner, Ute Rüegg, trained as a 'Special Detection Dog'. This takes scenting work to a very

Photo Ute Rüegg, Sweden

high level in the search for drugs, explosives and other materials. Isone has also trained in bed bug detection. Training takes a long time for the dog to achieve the highest levels of competence

Working in this sphere a dog might be required to search anything from a football stadium for explosives, a room for drugs, or a hospital for bed bugs.

Isone is described by Ute as being 'a very willing dog, independent and energetic, and most of all, very stable. She is not bothered by strange people or environments, new scents or noises.'

Undertaking a search means disregarding other scents and ensuring the whole of an area is covered thoroughly. The handler leads the search helping to ensure the dog does not miss any area. If the dog has a 'find' of what they are searching

Isone Uit't Holandse Entlinest (Photo Ute Rüegg, Sweden)

for, then she lies down at the spot where the find takes place.

In these situations, a dog has to work both confidently and independently and calmly maintain their concentration to the end of the work. These are all characteristics which an Entlebucher can ably demonstrate.

Isone and Ute have trained with Tina Krulle Ringfoss, TKR Detection Dog Center, www.tkrdetectiondogcenter.se in Sweden.

Breeding

Given the relatively low numbers of Entlebuchers worldwide and the small number of generations since the foundation dogs of the modern breed, as many dogs need to enter the breeding programme as possible. The high level of health testing, both in terms of cost and the number of dogs that are then excluded, makes things harder, but is entirely necessary. No responsible and caring breeder would want to risk breeding dogs with serious health conditions when these can be avoided. The danger is that, in the long run, excluding too many dogs will create its own risks to the breed due to reducing an already small gene pool. A fine balance between health and the gene pool needs to be maintained. Developing a global artificial insemination programme may be one way to do this and will be discussed later.

Every effort to encourage healthy dogs to breed needs to be taken. The difficulty here is that breeding is hard work, time consuming, costly and not for everyone. Because so many people who breed Entlebuchers do it for the good of the breed and are not experienced breeders, this section will provide some basic information which will help those coming to it for the first time. However, it is also worth buying and reading 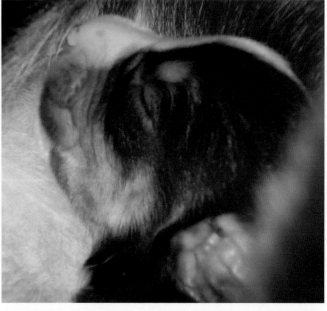 specialist books on breeding to learn more about the process as a whole. I still reread one that I have before every litter, to remind myself of all the little things I may have forgotten since the previous litter, such as the finer points of puppy CPR.

Breeding Entlebucher Mountain Dogs is the most rewarding thing I have ever done - it is also the most stressful. Being responsible for the lives of those tiny little dogs feels massive to me. Helping them to safely and happily reach the age of eight weeks old and be able to go on to bring so much joy to their families makes it all worthwhile. Meeting those dogs months or years later and being greeted by a welcome reserved only for the most special people in their lives is something you just can't beat.

Also be aware that no two dogs are the same and the experience of one breeder is not the experience of others. Even a breeder who has had many litters will be surprised from time to time by a completely new situation.

Never go into dog breeding with an eye on making money. Responsible breeding is expensive and it is not at all uncommon to lose money over the course of a whole breeding career.

Thankfully there are many Entlebucher breeders who provide a very high standard of care to both the bitch and the litter. When you add to that the health testing and putting the dogs through an Ankörung (breeding test) there are significant up-front costs. Similarly, as the breed is not widespread, in order to widen the gene pool it is quite common for the owner of the bitch to have to travel a significant distance to visit the stud dog. If you can face all of that, the resulting puppies will bring pleasure for many years to you and to their permanent homes.

With Torfheide Arnold (Arnie) Shadow's firstborn puppy

You should also be aware before embarking on breeding, that a responsible breeder will provide a lifetime commitment to all their puppies and should be prepared to take them back at any stage of their lives. An Entlebucher will never forget his breeder and even when it is years since he last saw you he is likely to roll on his back in submission and ecstasy the moment he smells your scent.

It is common within the breed for the first litter by a breeder to be their 'A' litter, their second to have names beginning with the letter 'B' and so on through the alphabet. Many highly respected kennels in Switzerland have been through the alphabet more than once. Although in the past sometimes the same name was used as in a previous litter, repeats of names within a kennel are no longer allowed. In the UK breeders have tried to avoid using any name which has been used by any other UK Entlebucher breeder, making it even easier for dogs to be referred to. This does not stop a new family giving their dog a pet name of their choice, but at least the kennel names are sufficiently different. That of course will get harder as more dogs are born in the UK.

In Belgium, the practice of choosing the starting initial for the names of a litter is different. Starting with 2001 as 'A' the letter is chosen according to the year of birth. Thus my eldest dog, born in Belgium in 2005, is Einstein van de Tiendenschuur, although at home he is known as Alfie.

Not all countries follow the naming conventions, but it is a nice touch and is certainly useful if trying to see which dogs are from the same litter.

Seasons

The 'season' or 'heat' is a key part of the reproductive cycle of a bitch. It is the time that the bitch's body is preparing for ovulation and the hormonal changes required for her to become pregnant. I could write a whole book on the subject of bitches and their seasons. Above all else, do not expect them to happen at convenient times or to happen like clockwork. An Entlebucher bitch's first season usually occurs at around the six to eight month mark. However, it can be as early as around four months of age or as late as nine months or more. A first season can also be very light and almost 'silent', or barely noticeable, in nature.

If you plan to breed from your bitch, then do keep a complete record of timings. Also note down other useful information. Around six to eight weeks prior to the start of her season a bitch will shed her coat. This can happen within the space of a few days, leaving what seem

The Torfheide 'C' Litter

like handfuls of fur everywhere. It is relatively short-lived, but the timing is worth noting as it is the best indicator you will have when you start trying to plan your diary around mating your dog. Once her season starts, her coat will come back thick and glossy. In the interim period she can look a little 'moth-eaten' and in particular might have a very 'thin' looking tail and a brown tinge to her coat. If you are showing your dog during this time she is unlikely to do well! If you are undertaking her Ankörung during this time, then it is worth making the judges aware that she is in her pre-season phase.

If you are keeping notes for breeding, include in your records which day the bitch starts bleeding, when the discharge becomes clear rather than red and any particular days that a male dog is very interested.

After their initial season, bitches tend to settle into some sort of pattern. This is most likely to be something around six monthly, but not necessarily and is rarely precise. After a litter, a season may be delayed, sometimes by as much as the

normal period of gestation. This is not something to be alarmed by.

If you are not planning to breed from your bitch, then of course neutering is an option. However, it is generally thought best to allow a dog to reach at least some degree of maturity first, for the benefit of her overall health. The body's hormonal development is closely connected to many areas of the body and its impact should not be underestimated. It is best to discuss this with your vet.

Seasons are inconvenient. Around the house they can be managed with the help of dog pants, however going out and about is much more troublesome. The safest option is not to take your bitch out from the first sign of her season for about four weeks. In reality, long before the end of four weeks, both you and she are likely to be going slightly crazy. You can occupy her during this time with increased use of puzzles and mind games, training etc, but there is no substitute for good exercise. However safe the environment may seem, it is very unwise to let her off the lead during this time. Her reaction through the phases of her season will vary and I'll come back to that in a moment, but it is not uncommon for her to develop wanderlust! Also, when she is in season, the pheromones she will secrete may not be obvious to a human but to a dog that has not been castrated they will carry on the wind for significant distances, much further than where you perceive to be a 'safe zone' which you can see with the naked eye. I can tell you from personal experience that a dog which has got the scent of an in season bitch is very difficult to dissuade! If you are going to walk her at this time then drive her away from your house so you don't have dogs 'calling' on her. Also, in fairness to the owners of other dogs do not take her to places that are popular for walking. A male dog can be very hard to control if he gets the scent of a girl, even if he is being walked many hours later.

As her season approaches, a bitch, particularly a young one, may be very playful. She will often then go through a phase where she is a little snappy around dogs if they try to sniff her rear-end in the time she is not ready to mate. When she does reach her fertile time, if you have other dogs around, even castrated ones, or other bitches, she may show her desperation to mate through play and overt demonstrations of what she is hoping for. An interesting home test of whether she is ready to mate, other than her writing it in capital letters, is to scratch her lower back and see if she lifts her tail to the side. There is more information on knowing when a bitch is ready to mate in the sections later in this book on progesterone and mating.

She will only be prepared to receive a stud dog for a limited number of days, once this time has passed a bitch may be a little snappy around other dogs again. Once her season has apparently finished an owner should wait at least a week to ten days before resuming normal activities as the bleeding stops some time before her ability to become pregnant does!

A bitch's seasons run through her whole life unless she is neutered.

Choosing a Stud Dog

It is worth noting that, due to the small gene pool and the relatively low numbers of dogs qualified for breeding, it is not usually possible to have an especially wide choice of stud dog. Matching the health tests and the level of inbreeding must be considered and after that there are rarely a large number of stud dogs to choose from. The pool of possible stud dogs is of course greater the further the bitch's owner is prepared to travel. Under normal circumstances, it is the bitch, rather than the stud dog, who does the travelling.

Siro v. d. Untergass (Photo Serge Renggli)

Health Tests

It is essential that these are looked at first. Unless the bitch is clear for PRA then the first consideration is to ensure that the stud dog is clear. After that, cataracts, gonio tests and ectopic ureter need to be looked at (see the health section for explanations). In all these matters and in the mate selection itself, assistance is available through the breed clubs. Consideration needs to be given to the individual requirements of the countries in which both the bitch and stud dog reside, as these vary for what is acceptable on health matches. That is not to say that any country is either right or wrong with regards to these conditions. We are all trying to work with the best available information, but with much not yet known about patterns of inheritance. Although we are learning all the time, there are still areas that our best understanding today may be disproved tomorrow. On the whole, the breed clubs try to work together to add to the knowledge available, but with language barriers and different research programmes this is not always easy.

Hip testing is a more straightforward consideration than the other areas as there are fewer requirements on which dogs can be matched as long as both have results at a good enough standard for the Club's requirements.

Temperament

Queenie's Character Test in Switzerland

Although in many countries dogs which have joined the breeding programme will have undertaken a character test to ensure that their temperament is suitable for breeding, there will still be a range of different characters within the breeding community. For example, some dogs are much closer to their original driven work ethic than others. If the puppies are being looked for essentially as pets, then it may be best to mate such a dog with one of a more laid-back temperament. This may come out in other ways. The nature of our breed is that they are normally naturally wary of strangers

until those people are accepted as part of the pack. However, there are wide variations in this and even among my own dogs they range from one who would rarely let a stranger anywhere close to the house unless told it was ok, to one who would invite them straight in and pour them a drink before asking the stranger's name.

Ramos Roxi v. Kornried (Photo Serge Renggli)

Thinking about the temperament of the dog to be mated and trying to offset any extremes of character can be very advantageous.

Physical Characteristics

No dog is perfect. Of course, some come pretty close and an 'excellent' in an Ankörung (breeding test) is something to be very proud of. However, when selecting a stud dog, there may be times when it is best to choose one to help address a minor conformation issue that has surfaced in a line. This can be as basic as a tendency to have longer white socks, or as critical as a tail with a tendency to curl further than ideal. The latter being a potential eliminating fault in both breeding and showing. The more you get to know the different breeding lines, the more you become aware of which lines carry a gene that expresses a particular feature such as a kinked tail, white patches, or misshapen ears for example.

Genetics

It is important to consider the level of inbreeding in the dogs. The gene pool of the breed is still relatively small and there are very few generations to get back to the foundation stock. By looking at each mating, breeders can do their best to broaden the gene pool, which in turn should assist in the long-term health and sustainability of the breed. One problem that can arise is when looking at only the very recent generations, it is possible to think that the inbreeding coefficient is very low. Due to the very recent development of the breed, if you look at only a few more generations the figures can be significantly different. However, working to keep inbreeding as low as possible over five generations is a good starting point. Normally one would expect the inbreeding coefficient (COI) to be below 5% but ideally much lower. In the UK we try to ensure that it is below 2.5% over five generations. Whilst this can be calculated manually or a rough approximation made by reference to the five generation pedigrees of the dogs, it is far better to use one of the computer programmes such as Zooeasy or Breedmate. Thankfully, some of the breed clubs have developed databases of many generations of dogs, which make reference to this information much easier and is one of many reasons why working through your breed club is in the best interests of good breeding.

It is not simply about mathematics. Breed knowledge builds up over time and suggests that it is worth looking back more generations to minimise the repeats of dogs that were prolific studs in the past.

Availability

Last but by no means least will be to find if the stud dog is available and to obtain permission through the responsible club. This is not something which can be left until the last minute and in normal circumstances it should be arranged at least a couple of months before you expect the bitch's season to start. It is then worth the owners of the two dogs staying in close contact to make sure that neither one's circumstances change.

Ustinov v. Rickental (Photo Serge Renggli)

Remembering that every mating is the creation of a new family and that the owner of the stud dog is likely to care about the outcome of the litter, and the ongoing lives of the puppies, is important. It can be the beginning of a good friendship between the owners of the dogs and it is always good if the breeder keeps the stud owner informed on the progress of the puppies.

Elio v. Schärlig (Photo Serge Renggli)

Progesterone Levels

Progesterone levels are essential in mating a bitch. Especially if you have long distances to travel, knowing at what point she is going to be ready to receive the stud dog is of critical importance. However, no two dogs are the same and in my experience from my own dogs, from talking to other owners and from tracking progesterone levels in relation to mating, the Entlebucher may follow a slightly different pattern than your vet will expect. None of that makes it easy.

It is also important to understand that a bitch's hormones follow the same pattern whether or not she is pregnant. This helps in explaining three things. Firstly, it is not possible to use a simple urine test to see if a bitch is pregnant. Any urine test relies on the changing hormone levels in order to provide an indication of pregnancy. Secondly, phantom pregnancies are not uncommon, whether or not the bitch has been mated. Thirdly, you cannot easily tell by changing behaviours that your bitch is pregnant.

Progesterone testing in its simplest form will tell you if your bitch has ovulated. This is of little use if you have a thousand miles to drive to the stud dog. Planning your journey is a difficult thing at the best of times. If you have kept a complete and accurate log of your bitch's seasons then you will have a broad idea of when you can expect the season to start. This may be as variable as anything from 23 to 35 weeks, even with the same dog, which makes planning your social calendar or making arrangements for being away from home somewhat challenging. This is where a knowledge of how many weeks before her season starts a bitch will shed her coat can be incredibly useful. It can act as your six to eight week warning bell and allow you to give reasonable notice to the stud dog owner.

Although expensive, for a bitch who has not been successfully mated before, it is useful to run a series of progesterone tests over the course of the season prior to the planned mating. By testing every other day through the course of the season from day one, you gain a picture of your bitch's progesterone level changes and an idea of how many days into her season she will be before she ovulates.

Norfolkfields Bella (Photo Sarah Fulker)

Do bear in mind that each bitch is different and getting to know what works for your own Entlebucher is more important than any textbook advice. For example, it is common to read suggestions of mating the bitch every other day through the critical period for around three matings. However, I do know of a number of Entlebuchers who would not stand for the stud dog for that range of time. If you can agree with the owner of the stud dog that the dogs can have three matings then you may be best for those to be three consecutive days, for example Monday, Tuesday and Wednesday, and not to include rest days between them.

In terms of the progesterone levels, please bear in mind that what follows is based only on my experience. Testing of progesterone levels in a dog is by blood sample. It is important to understand there are two different scales on which the progesterone level is measured. If some of your testing is at one vet and due to travelling, some at another, potentially in a different country, then do make sure you are working to the same scale. For reference one is 'nanomole' or 'nmol' and the other is 'nanograms per millilitre' or 'ng/ml' (ng is often the abbreviation and will be used below). At low levels, a reading may seem not dissimilar on both scales but that changes as they increase.

In the early part of a season, the reading will be below 1ng. Seasons can stop altogether at this stage and any particular stress to the dog may lead to the season not continuing as expected. Only when the progesterone level passes 2.5ng is it unlikely to decline and the season should continue normally. If you have a long journey to undertake, this can be a very important piece of information, as travelling to strange places prior to this may cause stress. Having travelled with a dog who has had what is called a 'split season' where the progesterone level dropped for a period of time before going back up, leaving me with the expense of staying away from home for an extended period, this is worth bearing in mind. I am also led to believe it is quite common in a split season for the bitch not to ovulate, making the whole trip futile, which it was in my case on that occasion.

Ovulation takes place at around 5ng. From testing results over a number of Entlebucher litters, mating is usually successful the second day after the progesterone level hits 3.5ng and then the day or two days after that. It is now thought that the best mating day will be two days post-ovulation. Ovulation may be anything from day 7 to day 17 (and quite possibly earlier or later still) of the season depending on the bitch.

It is particularly hard to assess the start of a season in some bitches as they may bleed very little, especially in the early days. This is where getting a base line from progesterone testing can be helpful to have a clearer idea of what to expect.

As already mentioned, phantom pregnancies can occur whether or not a bitch

Max v. d. Auenrüti and Shadow

is mated. I've had a bitch who has been mated be quite certain she is pregnant and behave like a princess for most of the normal time of gestation. I've also known of a bitch go through the full stages of pregnancy from going off her food to producing milk without having been mated at all. They may also start to produce milk if another bitch is in whelp in the house, which can be helpful if there is a large litter to feed, of course.

Mating

If you are planning to mate your dog and are unfamiliar with the process, then do seek out videos and information on the subject or assistance from within the breed club first.

Before you mate your bitch, make sure she is as fit as possible for the hoped for pregnancy. Now is not the time for her to be carrying extra weight. Also check her vaccinations are up to date to minimise having to give anything unnecessary during gestation and whelping. If you are travelling abroad to mate the bitch then she is likely to be wormed as part of her homeward travel if this is under the Pet Passport Scheme, if not discuss with your vet the optimum time to administer worming treatment to give the best start possible to the pups. If giving the canine herpes vaccine, which is highly recommended, this is administered to the bitch once during her season and again a couple of weeks before whelping. Discuss the exact timings with your vet. This vaccine helps to prevent puppy mortality as a result of canine herpes.

For some Entlebuchers, the close bond they form with their human seems to be an obstacle to mating. I have known more than one instance where the absence of the prime carer is better for mating to take place. This may be for a whole range of reasons, but it is something to bear in mind. For most dogs, when the timing is right, nothing much that you do will stop them! However, ensuring that you are quiet and calm and do not disturb or distract the dogs will help to ensure things run more smoothly.

Partly depending on how ready the bitch is, the dogs may play for anything

Rino v. d. Untergass and Shadow

from a second or two to half an hour before mating. If nothing has happened in this time, then you may need to try the following day if you are in the early part of the cycle.

It can be quite entertaining watching a novice stud dog trying to work out exactly what to do. Even more so when the bitch is experienced and is doing absolutely everything in her power to tell him. They do not need human help with this. They will work it out!

When the dogs do come together, the semen passes into the bitch quite quickly, however further fluid passes into the bitch which is believed to help the semen on its way and this occurs during the 'tie', at which point the stud dog will be back to back with the bitch and the bulbus glandis of the stud dog's penis is locked inside the bitch by her muscles tightening around it. This can last for anything from a couple of minutes to well over half an hour. If the dogs try to pull apart during this time it can lead to serious injury to one or other (or both) animals. It is a process which only happens in dogs and not in any other animal species. At this point, both the owner of the stud dog and the bitch should be on hand to gently, but if necessary firmly, hold their dogs in place. For some it is no more than being there to sooth and calm the dog if they become restless. At the extreme it is a question of almost holding the bitch in a body-lock to prevent her from moving. From my own experience, may I recommend taking a change clothes with you in case you need them before driving home! Finding yourself covered in dog body fluids with a long journey ahead can be disconcerting to say the least…

Binto-Sämi v Grundsteigeli and Shadow

Once the tie has completed, it's time to take a photo for the family album and wait to see if the mating has been successful. Getting your bitch to put her paws up is no bad idea at this stage. Of course, she needs to exercise and to stay fit, but don't take any chances you wouldn't take with human pregnancy.

Also ensure that at the time of mating all paperwork is completed that needs the signature of the stud dog owner to enable the registration of the puppies.

Artificial Insemination (AI)

Given the relatively small gene pool and the wide distribution of the breed, artificial insemination would appear to be a good option. However, for a number of reasons this has not been the case so far in Europe.

Many of the European clubs are not keen on the use of AI in breeding and will not give permission for its use. In some countries, there are rules which restrict the breeding of any progeny born through AI to ensure that no breed relies on it due to natural matings being impossible. However, in research undertaken by the American Club (NEMDA) some years ago, no successful pregnancies were achieved through the use of chilled or frozen semen. At the time, the conclusions which were reached meant that work in this area appeared to be too difficult to progress. Further research using different dogs has since had successful results using chilled semen and it appears that the conclusions reached from early research may not have given the whole picture.

There have also been successful results with AI on a side-by-side basis, where both dogs are present at the clinic at the same time, and the semen does not require chilling.

Significantly more testing will be needed before any firm conclusions can be drawn. Due to the cost of AI, until testing has more convincing results, it will remain the choice of last resort.

In an ideal world, with such low numbers of the breed, a semen bank would be created from good healthy stud dogs so that they could be used in the future. This might also enable owners who do not ultimately want to keep an uncastrated male to do so for long enough for his tests to be completed and for him to deposit semen for the future. It would also enable the easier exchange of breeding lines across much longer distances. However, such a project would need international support and would not be easy to set up.

Temperament of a Stud Dog

Keeping a stud dog is not for everyone but is an important part of developing the breed. It is essential that as many different dogs go on to mate as is practically

possible in order to broaden the gene pool across the generations. The owner will need to undertake the same level of health testing on their dog as on a breeding bitch, but of course unless the owner is also the bitch's owner they do not have the work of raising puppies to contend with. It does not necessarily make the ownership of a stud dog an easier option.

A question which is often asked is 'Does castrating my dog change his temperament?' The response is not straightforward.

Giro v. Bogenthal (Photo Serge Renggli)

Essentially, the answer is 'no' but there are caveats. Firstly, a castrated dog is less likely, though will still be tempted, to run off for a long distance on the scent of an in-season bitch. Secondly, a dog being kept for stud will be a happier dog if he does have chance to mate at regular intervals. Whilst some dogs have a moderate sex drive, others will be frustrated if that urge is not fulfilled. In a breed with few breeding bitches, it can be that the opportunities to mate are more limited and for some dogs that can become more of a problem for the owner to manage. In situations where the sex drive of the dog is leading to more displays of dominance, one option can be to provide him with an artificial means of release every few months and some dogs will do this for themselves. However, this is the point at which many owners will go down the route of castration as a permanent answer to the problem.

Thankfully, the above is not the case with all dogs who are kept for stud and some are, apparently, easier to manage than others.

Gestation

The standard gestation period of a litter of puppies is around 63 days. This is measured from the day the bitch ovulates rather than the day she is mated. Commonly, mating takes place after ovulation and so a litter may be born in

slightly fewer days than this from the date of mating. If anything, Entlebucher litters seem to arrive on the early rather than the late side.

The normal litter size in the breed is between four to six puppies. However, I am aware of litters with only one pup or as many as thirteen.

As the hormone pattern is similar even if a bitch is not pregnant, it can be difficult to judge if she is in whelp, particularly with a first litter. An ultrasound scan at around 35 days will generally provide an answer, however it is unlikely to tell you exactly how many puppies are present and may not always provide a clear enough picture to be certain either way. If you are the proud expectant human, there is nothing quite like seeing the little heartbeats on the ultrasound monitor

and coming away clutching the image of the results. By her third pregnancy, Shadow seemed to quite understand what was going on and was herself watching the screen to see her pups. It was a precious moment.

Where there is uncertainty from the ultrasound scan, or you need a more accurate idea of numbers (for example if the litter may be a single pup and therefore a caesarean may be more likely as the pup could be larger) then an x-ray much closer to

Shadow looking at the ultrasound of her third litter

full term is the best option. Even then you can spend many hours counting and recounting spines or heads in an attempt to work out exactly how many puppies there are.

Some books suggest that you move the bitch over to puppy food in the later stages of pregnancy for a number of good reasons. However, be careful. Puppy food has a much higher fat content and given some Entlebuchers seem to have a tendency to pancreatitis, moving onto puppy food can have disastrous consequences. The impact of the puppy food over time left Shadow very unwell and me hand-rearing her puppies while as a result she had treatment. As long as the bitch has a good healthy diet there is no reason to change it. There are excellent supplements such as 'Fit and Fertile' http://www.fitandfertile.com/ which can be given to the bitch from the time her season starts in a planned mating, right through to the whelping of her litter. I give it mixed with a spoon of vanilla yoghurt (having checked that the yoghurt contains nothing harmful to dogs such as xylitol) and they love it. You can also give the bitch calcium as a supplement for the appropriate period of time. There are also guides which will tell you how much to increase the bitch's food by as her pregnancy progresses. How strictly you need to follow this may depend on how greedy your bitch is. There is a fine balance between receiving enough nutrition to feed a litter of fast developing pups and putting on additional kilograms that will make the whole process harder work.

As the expected date of confinement approaches don't be shocked if your bitch stops eating. At the point you expect her to need the most energy as she gets ready to give birth she may well not eat for several days. The first time this happened I was extremely worried and cooked every tasty morsel that might tempt Shadow to eat. Thankfully by her second pregnancy I had learned that this was normal and, whilst keeping a careful eye on her, I at least stopped panicking.

As the time gets close, the bitch may find getting comfortable difficult, particularly if she is having a large litter. She will of course welcome back massages and tummy rubs at this stage, but will also appreciate an extra cushion or two. If you want to hear the puppies' heartbeats you can use a hand-held ultrasound doppler but it is quite hard to get a good connection through fur. As her time of giving birth approaches, she will lose most of the hair from around her teats ready for feeding the pups.

Whelping

Breeding books will tell you that some bitches like to give birth without any human interference and no human company. If you can find an Entlebucher who prefers to be in a room on her own then I would be very surprised. In the same way that as a breed they want to share every moment of their day with you, the birth of their puppies is a time they very much want their closest human to be present. If their human tries to leave the preferred whelping area at this stage they are likely to be followed and find the birth occurring wherever they are!

However, this is also a time when their dislike of strangers will come to the fore and in general they will not welcome the birth being treated as a spectator sport. They need an area which is calm and quiet and without too much coming and going.

Your bitch will need a whelping box in which to give birth. Measure the bitch from nose to tail and ensure the box will give her room to lie fully stretched out. In the UK, because the breed is still relatively unknown, relying on the description of a whelping box as being suitable for 'medium' sized dogs or dogs of a certain weight does not take into account the fact that this breed is longer in the body than most breeds of an otherwise similar size. Your bitch needs to be able to lie completely comfortably so she can expose all her teats to feed the pups.

According to the recent report 'Factors influencing litter size and puppy losses in the Entlebucher Mountain Dog' (see references) the average litter size is 5.49 puppies, which is reduced to 5.08 puppies by the time of registration, with losses running at 7.4%. The research has been based on registrations in Germany. They are very similar to figures collected by NEMDA (the American Club) of US born litters. Of the 12 litters born so far in the UK the average litter size is 5.9 puppies including stillborn pups. The total figure of 7% of early deaths matches the UK experience, where this has been essentially through still births and those where a

problem occurs during the birth. As yet in the UK, there have been no early deaths through later accidents (such as the mother rolling on a puppy).

It is also interesting to consider survival rates by birth weight. The following figures have been collected by looking at the records for a number of litters:

Under 200g birth weight, an Entlebucher puppy has a survival rate of under 10%.

Puppies with a birth weight of under 300g still

only have a 50:50 chance of survival, whereas those born at over 450g have a very high survival rate.

This is not the right place to tell you all you need to know about the whelping process. If you are going to breed from your dog, then learn as much as you can ahead of time. Learn how to take your bitch's temperature and keep a record of what it is normally. Start taking it regularly around a week before the puppies are due. Roughly 12 to 24 hours before she is due to give birth, there will be a sudden sharp dip in her temperature and if you can recognise when this is it will help you to be completely ready. This is another area where bitches can differ, so knowing what is 'normal' for your dog is of more value than a textbook specified figure.

Stage 1 of labour will find the bitch creating a nest for herself, ideally where you have chosen, but just as probably if you do not keep an eye on her it can be under a bush in the garden or on the settee. There may be some low level contractions at this stage and some panting. She is very likely to be restless and have difficulty settling. This can go on for some time. In the case of Shadow's first litter it was a couple of very sleepless days and nights.

Stage 2 labour is when the major contractions start and the birth is imminent. From here on, it is unwise to let the bitch out of your sight.

In advance of the birth, your preparation should include not only what to expect for the actual birth process, but also how to undertake CPR on a new-born puppy and even more importantly how to help clear fluid from the lungs. That last point is needed quite regularly and can be the difference between losing a puppy or being able to watch him grow to maturity.

If you want to see an actual Entlebucher birth, then I managed to video some of Shadow's first litter and you can find these, together with videos of them growing up, on Youtube https://youtu.be/Cwpuh9CanV0

Suggested Equipment

Whelping box – size approx. 40″ (102cm)

Newspaper – to go in the base of the whelping box / pen - remove any staples in advance (broadsheets are best)

Heat pad – ideally set up in separate pen. This enables any new-born pups to be moved out of the way when the bitch is in the final stages of giving birth to the next one, as well as being useful when the bitch needs to go out over the next few days. While the birth is taking place it is best for the pups to be with the bitch as much as possible as their suckling and her washing them will not only be to their benefit but will help to stimulate contractions for the next pup.

Pen – apart from a small separate pen to contain the pups when they are on the heat pad and for when you are cleaning out the main whelping box, it is worth having a much larger pen for the puppies to move to at three weeks old, when they are ready to play and are busy learning how to climb out of the whelping box.

Vet bed – you will need several pieces of vet bed or old sheets to go in the whelping box over the newspaper. It must be the breathable type and not the one with rubber back. It is very good at letting any liquid pass through while staying relatively dry on the surface, the newspaper underneath will absorb the moisture. You may want some non-slip vet bed to have outside the whelping box for the times the bitch gets out and for you to kneel on when tending to the pups. A gardening 'kneeler' can be very useful for this too.

Forceps – to clamp cords.

Surgical single use scissors – to cut cords.

Iodine – to disinfect.

Cotton wool – for the iodine application.

Cotton / dental floss – to tie cords if necessary.

Nasal aspirator – to clear nose and throat of puppy.

Stethoscope – to listen for heartbeats.

Flannels – several.

Towels – lots.

Thermometer – to take the bitch's temperature.

KY jelly - for the thermometer.

Torch - this is very useful if the bitch finds a dark corner or is turned with her head toward you at the time of birth. A head torch or one that has a stand will keep your hands free.

Hand sanitiser

Animal disinfectant – several bottles. Cleaning out the whelping area daily will considerably reduce the risks of infection to the puppies.

Cleaning cloths

Scales – must be stable. Whilst a very young puppy does not wriggle much, as they grow weighing them becomes more difficult. Specialist baby scales can be a good option.

A small pet carrier – for taking the puppies to the vet for checks etc. Depending on the number of puppies in the litter you may need more than this as the weeks pass if you wish to transport them all at the same time.

Empty plastic bottles (1.5 or 2 litre) – these can be filled with warm water and wrapped in towels to act as hot water bottles for any pups you need to take in the carrier to the vet. Their shape makes them more inviting to snuggle up to for the puppies to stay warm.

Feeding bottles – there is a set by Royal Canin with multiple sizes of teat, these can work well as the puppies grow if you need to supplement their feeding.

Sterilising tablets – whilst a 'Whelping pack' is likely to include them, the bitch is going outside regularly for the toilet and to stretch her legs, so it is impossible to provide pups with a sterile environment.

To make some of these items easy to find, I have set some of them up with links to buy them here http://alfiedog.me.uk/we-recommend/

You should also have prepared your car in advance in case the bitch needs emergency transport to the vet during the birth process. Ensure you have covered a seat with newspaper and have clean towels available. Ideally travel with a passenger who can stay with the bitch in case she starts giving birth while you drive. This is particularly relevant if the vet administers an oxytocin injection to induce labour. You may have a relatively short time from the injection being administered to the next puppy arriving. Be warned!

New-born Pups

Most bitches will do all the work that is needed for the birth without your intervention. However, ensuring you are familiar with the process and what might be needed if a puppy is stuck, as well as how long to leave the bitch between puppies before calling for help, will be the difference between life and death for some of the pups. If possible, attend a birth prior to your own bitch giving birth, or have an experienced breeder on hand for your first litter. It is always worth having a second pair of hands helping you, as when intervention is needed it can be needed quickly and help may be required at those times.

What you will need to be prepared for, even if the birth is an easy one for the bitch, is to cut any long ends of umbilical cord she may leave, or to tie any cords which are not sealed off properly and are bleeding. Whilst genetic umbilical hernias can occur in the breed, they are as commonly caused by an over-enthusiastic bitch cutting the cord too close. Sterile dental floss can come in handy to close off a leaking umbilical cord, or at the extreme a line of cotton. You will also need good eyesight and ideally someone else to hold the pup, particularly if your hands are shaking as you try to do it.

You may also need to remove any birth fluid from the nose and mouth of pups and to help by gently rubbing them to stimulate them into life if the bitch is busy with giving birth to the next pup. The need for you to assist is more likely if the puppies are born close together. Most bitches will wash the new-born pup vigorously themselves. Also make sure each new-born pup has the opportunity to suckle as soon as possible as they can only absorb the antibodies from the colostrum for a few hours (up to about eighteen hours) following birth.

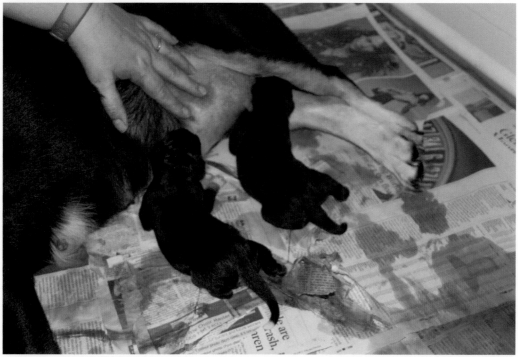

Once labour is complete, it is best to have both the bitch and all the pups checked by a vet to make sure there are no serious defects in the pups and that there are no pups retained by the bitch. Try to book this at the end of busy clinic hours both to reduce the time the pups are away from heat and to keep them clear of risks of infection.

In early life, a puppy cannot regulate his temperature and needs to be provided with external warmth from the bitch or another heat source until he can. It is a fine balance between heating the whelping room to a warm enough temperature for the safety of the pups and the bitch ending up too warm. In that regard, it is definitely easier to have a summer litter rather than a winter one, when the heating bills can become costly. As the puppies reach the stage where they can regulate their temperatures, the room temperature can gradually be reduced to more normal levels.

The main causes of death to puppies in very early life are being rolled on by the mother, chilling, infection and a non-visible defect.

As soon after birth as possible, weigh the puppies. Add this information to all other birth information about the litter, such as the time of birth, whether the puppy was breached, whether he has dew claws etc.

Some people refer to the new-born puppies as 'Puppy 1' 'Puppy 2' and so on. I can't bring myself to do that. As each one enters the world, he receives a name. I spend many pleasurable hours coming up with the names our puppies will have and by the time of the births these are listed in the priority order for boys and for girls. Once they have been identified I know exactly what their name will be.

It is hard to see the markings on new-born pups. One of the most amazing things about bringing up a litter of puppies is watching their shape and markings developing day by day. It is very easy in the first few days to worry that your whole litter has marking faults, misshapen heads or disproportionately sized ears - because these all develop at different rates.

Initially the brown fur can, in places, be hard to differentiate from the black, but within the first few days minor changes begin and white starts to appear too. It is very common to find at least a patch of white hairs on one of the shoulders, a throwback to the gene which gives rise to a neck-ring of white hair. However, this will often reduce as the puppy grows and may disappear altogether. It can be very difficult indeed when the puppies are born to note down enough differences to ensure each pup can be accurately identified. Markings, dew claws, weight are all important factors in identifying individuals, as of course is the sex of the puppy.

One alternative is to use something like a coloured collar. In my experience, the bitch will remove anything I add to the puppy at this stage and even the suggestion of painting different coloured nail polish on each puppy's claws as an identifier, failed to work. If you weigh pups regularly their weight can be a very useful guide to who is who, unless several are relatively close. In a short period of time, in addition to the markings, you will be able to discern the developing personalities and it is fascinating to watch how differently they behave even at under three weeks old.

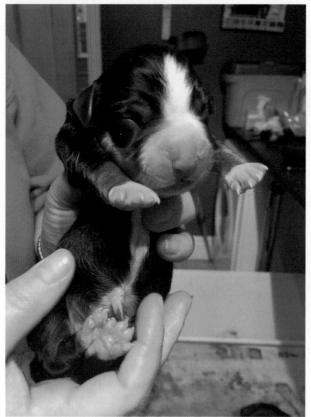

It is exciting in the early stages to watch the changes in their bodies as, for example, ears first become tiny flaps, then gradually fold over and start to develop into the shape we know and love.

As a complete novice with my first litter, I panicked about what looked like 'club' feet that had yet to develop into those beautiful Entlebucher paws and I had no understanding of the need for noses to be little snubs to enable the young animal to suckle on a teat. Over time the noses gradually extend and the colours of markings begin to show.

Torfheide Chekov (Otto) minutes after birth

I sat and watched the pups for hours as they went from looking like noseless moles to guinea pigs and onward into tiny dogs. Every day you can see changes as the rapid developments take place. The best moment is when their tails begin to wag as they contentedly find their meals.

New-born pups quite normally lose a little weight before they start gaining. It is worth keeping a chart so that you can be sure that all are increasing their weights at a steady and even rate after that, doubling in weight in their first week. Any variation in the pattern of an individual puppy should be monitored carefully. If the variation is in the rate of progress of the whole litter, then the first consideration is to check the health of the mother and ensure she is able to produce enough milk.

If the bitch does not have enough milk for any reason, or cannot feed the puppies then it is time to give supplementary food to the puppies. There are good formula products that can be used, but in my experience you are likely to run into

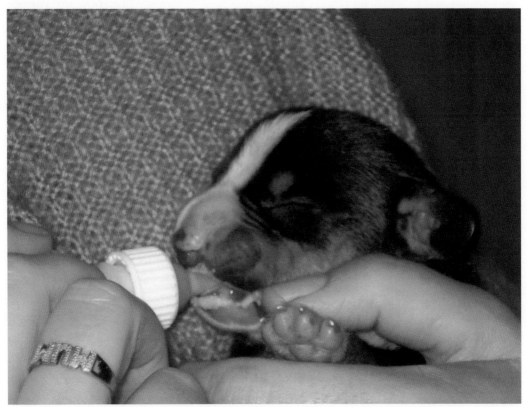

one of several problems. 1) Puppies suckle small quantities regularly. Particularly if you are feeding a large litter. By the time you finish feeding the last puppy you will have to start again with the first and unless you can get helpers you will get no sleep at all. 2) Using puppy formula milk does not give the same degree of protection against puppy cataracts as the bitch's milk will do. 3) I have never found a formula that the puppies like!

When I was faced with an emergency situation of having to hand rear pups I was advised to try the following:

• 1/3 cup of strong homemade beef broth (best made with liver)
• 1 can Evaporated Goat's milk (can substitute evaporated cow's milk) DO NOT DILUTE
• 1 cup of whole fat live culture yogurt (the higher the fat content the better)
• 2 raw egg yolks
• 1 Tablespoon Hellman's mayonnaise (which does not contain some of the additives of other products) or canola oil
• 1 teaspoon Karo syrup or corn syrup, (any colour)
• 1 teaspoon of baby vitamins

It worked! Not only did the pups like it but they took it readily.

If you have to go down this route, it has a higher calorie level than powdered puppy milk, which means they need a smaller amount each mealtime and you can feed more pups in a shorter time. I am not an expert on puppy nutrition and cannot tell you why each of the ingredients is needed or what they add, but I can say that it saved the day for Shadow's puppies and I was very grateful.

Bear in mind that the puppy cannot, in the early stages of life, expel waste

without stimulation from the mother. If the mother is not available to do this then you can use a damp cotton wool pad, or flannel, to simulate the action of the mother's tongue to activate this process in the puppy. A gentle sweeping motion, up the lower abdomen from the genital area of the puppy will do this. As you observe each puppy starting to be able expel waste for themselves you will be relieved of that duty.

With the biggest risk of death through injury being the mother rolling on a puppy, it is worth having roll bars in the whelping box to reduce the likelihood of this happening. There is a stage where the bars themselves can become a risk and it is a tough decision when to remove them, made harder if there is wide variation in puppy sizes within a litter. By the time puppies reach one kilogram in weight, I breathe a sigh of relief that the risk from the mother is significantly diminished.

Entlebuchers are often born with dew claws. That is a claw which is not fully attached to the foot and jointed as a normal toe would be. Although dew claws are normal on front legs, some pups are born with rear dew claws. Where this happens, as these are often not properly joined, they are at risk of twisting or catching on things causing the dog pain or injury as it grows. In some countries, including the UK, it is normal to remove rear dew claws at between one and three days of age, when, although it does cause the pup some discomfort, they will recover quickly and do not require an anaesthetic. The alternative is to wait until the pup is around six months of age and remove them under a general anaesthetic which is far more difficult.

They may also be born with a second dew claw, on either the front or back paw and as with others that are not properly joined these are often best removed.

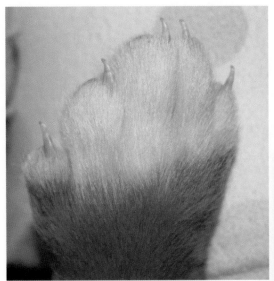

As with other breeds, it is normal for an Entlebucher to have four full normal clawed toes on each foot. However, one of my own litters of puppies included one pup with a full fifth clawed toe on each of his back paws, known as 'polydactyl'. I am

aware of one other in the breed where this has occurred. It is not uncommon in mountain dog breeds, some having more toes as a norm. It is not like a dew claw, it is a fully functioning toe and is perfectly healthy.

Entlebuchers historically were born with natural bob-tails. Some are still born with short tails even now, although it is increasingly uncommon. There are some people who suggest that the bob-tail is in some way detrimental to health, although I am unaware of this being supported by any case history. There are other schools of thought that eliminating the gene for short tails and thereby the dogs that go with it, is detrimental to the overall good of the breed and there may well be logic to that argument. However, given that docking is illegal in many countries, the bob-tail has fallen out of fashion, in part because of the rigmarole of having to prove it is natural and not docked. So far no puppies have been born in the UK with a bob-tail but it is potentially only a matter of time. Given that tail docking is illegal, if any puppies are born with short tails it is advisable for the breeder to have the Club undertake a control visit within the first few days to provide an official record of the litter. This should also be recorded by the breeder's vet.

Puppies are born with their eyes and ears closed. The breeder should ensure these areas are clean and that there is no discharge from either. Eyes and ears will both start to open at approaching the two week mark, eyes a little before ears. It is wonderful to be the first person a puppy sees and to watch him start to focus on his surroundings. Until this point he will have been totally driven by scent and used that sense to find both his mum and litter mates as well as, of course, the milk. Occasionally you may have a puppy with a less well developed sense of

Norfolkfields Bella (Photo Sarah Fulker)

smell and will find yourself constantly pointing him in the right direction as he searches fruitlessly around himself.

When the eyes do open they will be blue and only start to turn brown some weeks later.

At around two weeks old the puppy will be starting to stand, although falteringly at first. By three weeks he will be trying to walk around and soon after he will be ready to create havoc by trying to climb out of the pen!

Puppies are ready to start being weaned at around three weeks of age. One effective way to do this is to move them onto a puppy gruel made up of the formula substitute described above mixed with goat's milk, baby rice cereal and a tablespoon of plain organic yoghurt. This can start very thin so the pups can easily learn to lap the mixture. Once they have mastered this you can gradually vary the quantities to make it thicker by adding in baby food (ensuring it does not contain

onion!) and reducing the other ingredients, before moving them on to puppy food (well soaked if you are using a dry food) instead of the baby food. Gradually leave out the other ingredients and replace with water. Shadow's pups found the initial puppy milk substitute so tasty that they were not happy to have it taken away!

The puppies will still receive some milk from the bitch even as they move onto solid food, but the length of time she is prepared to feed them once their teeth have started to come through will be very much shorter. The puppies, once eating solid food, will also need access to water. This can be done more safely using a chicken feeder than in an open dish that a puppy could risk falling asleep in.

Allow the bitch to eat as much as she needs while she is lactating and then slowly reduce the quantity as she weans the pups. Once she stops feeding the pups it is time for her to go back to her normal maintenance level of food.

From three weeks old the puppies will be ready to start playing for very short periods of time after eating and before falling asleep. Sometimes at this stage they will fall asleep in the middle of playing. Now is the time to introduce toys which will stimulate the puppies to learn about different textures, sounds and movements. As you watch which pups prefer to play together, which will play on their own and which have a particular companion, you will start to see the personalities coming through. Don't be surprised if a puppy who marches straight over his brothers and sisters to get what he wants, is more dominant in later life, whereas a puppy who makes sure none of the others miss out at mealtime will continue to show more nurturing characteristics. My little Aristotle would always spend time looking around and taking everything in before going on to experience it. He is and always has been a thinker and I could not have picked a better name for him. Basil (Beethoven as he was first named), began rearranging the whole pen from about three and a half weeks old. He had mischief in his genes. It is wonderful to watch them all, but it also gives you important information when trying to match each dog to the right home.

In an Entlebucher, sometimes a tail curls further than desirable. This is a throw-back to the links with the Appenzeller in which the tail is expected to curl. In general the white of the tail would not normally do any more than just touch the back, if it reaches it at all. However, in some cases a tail curls far enough for the black on the tail to lie along the back when it has curled over. This is a fault and may affect a dog both in terms of joining the breeding programme and in the show ring. This often does not appear in a puppy until around 14 - 18 weeks of age and may occur much later. It is one of the many points on which it is absolutely impossible to give any guarantees of a puppy's suitability for breeding at a later date. Some dogs clearly carry the gene for tail curling. Over the course of four litters, almost half of Shadow's puppies have had tails with additional curl. I learned relatively early on that not only is it in her breeding line, but it is a gene which is fairly dominant. In choosing stud dogs it then became important to find dogs who had good tails in an attempt to help compensate for the trait.

Tails may also exhibit a kink at some point along their length. A breeder should

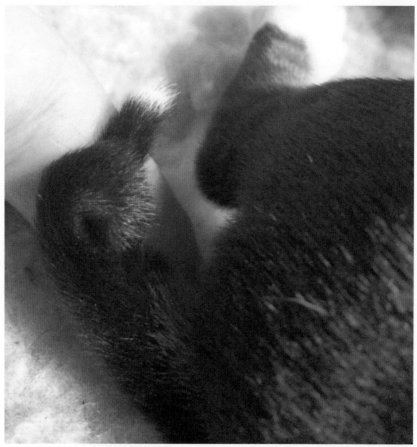

carefully run their fingers along the length of each tail as it develops to identify any knobbly bits. A kink can be as minor as a small deviation or as large as a complete change of direction. One of Shadow's puppies had a tail which was perfectly straight, then did a complete corkscrew before continuing straight.

THE ANKÖRUNG

Queen Viktoria Spod Hradze's (Queenie)
Conformation Test April 2010

The Ankörung is the name given to the Swiss Breeding Test. It is made up of three parts and is designed to ensure that all dogs which enter the breeding process are fit for the function they were originally bred to do. Although some aspects of the test have been adjusted over the years, it essentially looks for a dog that is still suitable to herd cattle and be able to face whatever tests of character and physical challenge come his way. The three parts, 1) health, 2) conformation to breed standard and 3) character, are explained in more detail below.

The test is run in Switzerland twice a year, in spring and autumn, and has been picked up to a greater or lesser degree by other national clubs within the breed. Germany, Austria and The Netherlands were the first to run an Ankörung outside Switzerland. It is also used in the USA, although it is not compulsory there. In the UK it was first run in 2013 and is designed to follow the Swiss model as closely as possible. Some countries use assessment and placing in Championship Dog Shows in place of the Ankörung, but this does not cover the character test or the level of detailed information on conformation recorded within the Ankörung paperwork.

Although the requirements may vary by country, a dog should be at least 18 months old to be entered in his Ankörung, although it is usually better to wait until he is around two years of age to give the maturity that the character test can require and to allow for his full exterior body development.

Conformation to Breed Standard / Exterior Test

In examining the conformation of the dogs, there are very detailed criteria for every aspect of their body, from height to eye shape, from musculature to coat markings. The assessment serves two clear purposes. Firstly, it ensures that the dog is suitably constructed for herding cattle many times its size. The dog must be agile and fast, but strong and solidly built. Secondly, the appraisal is intended to preserve the appearance of the breed, keeping it distinct from other breeds and true to the type that is so loved. Does it matter if an individual dog is missing one of its white socks? Probably not, but over time if that and other marking faults are allowed to perpetuate then the appearance becomes completely different. There are breeds which have changed in appearance significantly over the years, through fad and fancy, often driven by the show ring. Thankfully, the Entlebucher is not one that has changed and if you look at images of many of the early dogs they would be as comfortable attending a modern event and largely indistinguishable from their fellow dogs.

Cindarella v Ryffenbühl (photo Serge Renggli)

Some of the specific requirements do make more sense if you look at what have been the more common faults over the years. The specification that any patch of white on the nape of the neck should not be more than half a palm in size, for example, makes sense when you see the frequency with which white collars seem to resurface.

Only those dogs who are graded 'Excellent' or 'Very Good' in their conformation test are given permission to breed. Detail of the conformation assessment used in the UK can be found in the appendices.

If a dog does not pass an Ankörung, whilst he cannot be prevented from breeding, he cannot do so under the rules of the relevant Club and in some countries his puppies cannot be registered as pedigree. This is an important point to consider when looking for a mate from other countries.

Character Test

The character test subjects the dog to a range of experiences to gauge different reactions. It is essentially broken into three parts, although as a whole it also assesses the bond between dog and owner. An Entlebucher must be fearless, but not aggressive. He should have a sense of fun, but know when to stop. His bond with his human should be unshakeable, but he should not be unduly stressed when separated from his human.

The first section tests the dog's reactions around other people on both a crowd and individual basis. The assessment covers the dog's reaction as a crowd advances toward him whilst he stands with his human, as well as the reaction of the dog when his human is out of sight but there are other people around. Section one also looks at the willingness of the dog to play with both his own human and with a stranger.

A crowd advances toward the dog

In the second part, the dog is faced with different sensory stimulations. Whether they are auditory, visual, or textured the dog should not be fazed. He should be inquisitive, but not fearful. He should also be prepared to stay with his handler throughout the entire process, whether cow bells are rung, cans dragged along the floor, a sheet dropped in front of him, or if he is asked to walk across a strange surface. He may even be faced with an umbrella being thoughtlessly opened in his direction. This latter has been remarked on by some as being an odd test and unrealistic, but is one my own dogs have encountered when walking in public parks, when thankfully they were not put off from their stride.

In the final section of the character test the reactions of the dog are tested when a stranger approaches and also when an unknown dog approaches them. For these they are assessed both with their owner present and then while sitting quietly on their own.

A stranger approaches the dog and owner

It is possible for the dog to be asked to come back to repeat the character test if it is felt greater maturity is required before he can be passed. This may apply to some or all of the testing within the character section of the Ankörung.

Testing the character of an Entlebucher is a fine balance between him being fearless and yet reticent with strangers. In a working environment, the dog rarely has to deal with people outside of his immediate circle. Here he can remain slightly aloof from people who are not part of his pack without any detriment to his performance. However, he must not be put off by unexpected noise, movement etc and must continue the job in hand. Faced with each new stimulus it is good for him to be inquisitive in order to assess if his plans need to change as a result, but then he must continue with whatever task he is undertaking. As with a confident and balanced human, something may take a dog by surprise, but once a human gets a measure of what it is he continues as before and so must the dog.

The other key consideration in assessing the balanced Entlebucher is that he has formed a strong bond with his prime carer and will, even after diversions, return to his human's side and stay with him throughout the required exercises.

When parted from his human, an Entlebucher should not worry, but should remain alert and attentive for the owner's return, whilst at the same time being calm about what happens in the intervening period.

In all the activities with strangers, the dog should not show aggression at any point, even if he finds a situation stressful.

A detailed description of the character test is included in the appendices.

Health Tests

In order to receive permission to breed, a dog must have successfully undergone a number of health checks. The requirements for health vary by country with some tests being optional rather than compulsory. Essentially the key tests which are considered as part of breeding are set out below and explained in more depth in the health section of the book which follows:

Heart - this is a basic test to show the dog is free of any heart murmurs.

PRA (Progressive Retinal Atrophy - an eye condition which can cause blindness. To ensure that the correct matches are made in breeding and that no dog develops this condition, a DNA test must have been carried out on the dog to ascertain whether he is clear of the condition or is a carrier. This test is universally recognised as being essential.

Gonio test - this is a one-off eye test which is an indicator of the potential risk of developing glaucoma and is now asked for more often due to increased incidence of glaucoma.

Cataracts - another eye test but required annually. As to what is allowed, this varies by country and is explained in more detail on the health section of the book.

Hip dysplasia (imperfect hip joints) - an X-ray of the dog's hips must have been taken and assessed by the appropriate veterinary body. The way the score for the hips is expressed varies by country and there is more information in the section on health conditions.

Ectopic Ureter (incorrect positioning of the lines from the kidneys to the bladder) - this specialist ultrasound test is explained in more detail in the section on health conditions.

Some breeders undertake elbow dysplasia testing on their breeding dogs. However, as this is not a common condition in the breed, it is not generally a required test. Although its cause can be environmental rather than genetic, it would be unusual for a responsible breeder to breed from a dog which was known to suffer from this condition or any other condition that has the potential to have a genetic cause.

HEALTH INTRODUCTION

As with any dogs, there will be a range of conditions that an Entlebucher may encounter during his lifetime, but careful breeding helps to ensure that his life expectancy is a relatively good one.

What follows is a brief explanation of the conditions which are more common in the breed. This is not intended as a source for medical diagnosis and if you have any concern about the health of your dog then please consult your vet. Your dog should be registered with a vet from the first day he is with you and it is always wise to have an initial health check of your puppy as soon as you bring him home. This also serves to introduce him to the environment of the veterinary practice you will use when both he and you are calm and not concerned about any necessary treatment. A good breeder will have had the puppies fully health checked, but a follow up visit when he moves home is always recommended.

In choosing your vet, do ask around for recommendations in your area. In

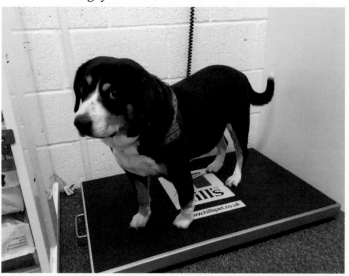

particular, if you plan to breed from your dog, ensure you choose a veterinary practice that will be supportive of that goal and who will be able to provide the out of hours cover you may need. It is not uncommon, particularly in cities, for vets to urge owners to have a dog neutered and discourage any breeding, without reference to the rarity of the breed and the need to keep the gene pool as broad as possible. If you plan to breed from your dog, a practice which is not supportive of that ambition is probably not the one to choose. A vet who themselves has experience in breeding can be invaluable.

What follows covers the major conditions for which tests may be required when breeding followed by other more common issues. Some breeders do test for Elbow Dysplasia but this is uncommon within the breed. As far as I am aware only around 2% of Entlebuchers are affected, including one of my own, Aristotle. However, as the condition can result from a number of factors, there is scant evidence of a genetic link. In my own dog it seems to have been injury related, but that's another story. I have also heard of shoulders being tested, but that is not a common test or problem within the Entlebucher breed as far as I am aware.

Do not alarm yourself reading the following sections and draw the conclusion that these are not healthy dogs. In general, the reason for the high degree of testing and awareness of conditions is to keep the breed healthy and ensure its strong future development. I have attempted to provide as thorough a discussion as possible of relevant issues as they can apply to Entlebuchers. Such conditions of course exist in all dogs, pedigrees and non-pedigrees alike.

I have not covered everyday issues and ailments. These should be discussed with your vet. Nor have I made specific mention of cancers as, thankfully, whilst these do occur, they do so only in the way they would in the general population and not with any breed specific tendency.

In keeping your dog healthy, feeding and exercise are important and have their own sections as do foods and plants which can be poisonous to a dog. Here I will make specific mention of sticks. I do not know any dogs who don't like sticks. However, I know several dogs who have had life threatening injuries as a result of getting splinters of wood from sticks into the soft tissue of the throat. Throwing sticks for a dog is incredibly dangerous and risky for your dog. If you have a dog who particularly likes this type of 'toy' then buy them a safe artificial stick to ensure they do not end up at the vet! Injuries of this sort are much more common than most owners realise.

The following section has been written as an introduction to the invaluable work being carried out in Zurich to gain a greater understanding of the health of the breed. I am grateful to Claude Schelling for sharing this insight.

HEALTH AND DISEASE IN ENTLEBUCHER MOUNTAIN DOGS
(an introduction by Claude Schelling, Klinik für Reproduktionsmedizin, Zurich, Switzerland.)

The controlling of inbreeding levels and inherited diseases have been in the focus of dog breeders during the last decades. High inbreeding levels might not only be responsible for reduced fertility, decreased vitality and monogenic recessively inherited diseases, but they may also contribute indirectly to the occurrence of some congenital anomalies, malformations and other inherited diseases.

The tremendous progress in the field of dog genetics allowed for the development of specific gene tests for numerous mutations segregating in domestic dog populations. Gene tests can be performed at any age of a dog and regardless of a clinical diagnosis. Especially in the case of recessively inherited diseases they are invaluable tools to select dogs as parents for the next generation without the risk that affected puppies are born. Without a gene test at hand, the big problem for breeders is to recognize carriers of the mutation which do not manifest the disease themselves. As a result, such dogs can transmit the mutation to the next generation before they are recognized to be a carrier. For the Entlebucher mountain dog, the progressive retinal degeneration (PRA) is an excellent example to demonstrate, how difficult the control of a recessively inherited disease is without an available gene test. To fight a single inherited disease when a gene test is available seems to be a rather simple task.

However, most dog breeders have to fight more than one "problem" in their populations. In this regard it should be emphasized that the terms healthy breed (few problems) or not healthy breed (more problems) should be avoided because they are not helpful in solving any of the problems. When the breeders have to deal not only with the guidelines of the breed standard but also with several health problems, it is wise to reflect and prepare a priority list of problems according to criteria like disease burden for an affected animal or the prevalence in the population. So controlling or fighting a disease might be a real challenge.

In addition, there are a lot of traits, diseases or predispositions for diseases which are not inherited in a simple Mendelian way like PRA. Their inheritance patterns are rather complex and their heritability is usually low or only moderate. Hip dysplasia is an excellent example of such a disease. The genetic background and the environment (food, activity) both render a certain level of liability for each dog to develop hip dysplasia. If a so called threshold level on the liability scale is surpassed, then the animal will develop hip dysplasia. The prevalence of such a disease then describes the rate of affected animals. This kind of inheritance is also often called multifactorial, because the genetics and the environment contribute both in varying degrees to the development of a disease. For such diseases, the selection based solely on the phenotype of an animal might not be the best solution. A sire with perfect hips might have more offspring with bad hips than a sire with slightly or moderately bad hips.

As an alternative, breeding values are often estimated by combining pedigree data with phenotypic data of a population. The breeding value of an individual dog is estimated by taking his own phenotype and the phenotypes of ancestors and offspring as well as all other relatives. This allows for the genetic ranking of an individual dog compared to his peers. Here it is important to understand, that a breeding value for a dog should always be given with its coefficient of determination. This means that breeding values which were estimated based on a lot of different phenotypical information from relatives of a single individual are more accurate (or closer to the true breeding value) than the ones which were estimated solely on the phenotypic performance of the individual.

An important issue is the compliance of the breeders. This means, that information of dogs with undesirable diagnoses or traits are not withheld and that the findings of the breeding value estimation have to be fully implemented when selection of breeding dogs is performed.

We are estimating breeding values for ectopic ureters and umbilical hernias. This is not an easy task, because not every Entlebucher mountain dog is tested.
Claude Schelling
Klinik für Reproduktionsmedizin
Zurich, Switzerland.
September 2017

Training Commands for Health Tests

Visits to the vet do not have to be as difficult as they often turn out to be. I have covered elsewhere the benefit of getting your dog accustomed to the vet before there is any need for treatment, but this can be taken several stages further by training your dog in what he will need to do when at the vet. My own dogs have some way to go in this department but that is because it is not something I had until recently thought to do.

Mine are taught commands such as **'Teeth'** for the times in the show ring that

they need to be happy for someone to move their gums away to see their teeth as well as 'Open' which is an essential command if you ever need to remove something from the mouth or look to the back of their throat. Shadow is also familiar with the need to **'Stand and Wait'** so I can take her temperature without her sitting on the thermometer. In a good puppy training class you will also learn to get your puppy to allow you to give him a full examination including his paws.

In addition to this many everyday commands can come in helpful such as:

Paw – to get your dog to give his paw to the vet for blood tests or examination.

This can also be useful after a walk when you need to dry each paw with a towel.

Mat – this is to get the dog to lie down in a relaxed fashion on a surface of your choosing, such as the vet's table.

Watch – to get your dog to focus on something and take his mind of what is happening. I also use 'to me' when I went them to look at me rather than for example a treat I'm holding.

Wait – is an obvious one while the vet is undertaking an examination or procedure.

Side or relax – can be taught when you want your dog to lie on his side rather than his tummy for examination.

Turn – is also a good idea to get the dog to voluntarily turn in the opposite direction.

Progressive Retinal Atrophy

Progressive Retinal Atrophy (PRA) is a range of conditions, associated with the eyes, in which the retina degenerates leading to blindness. It is not present in all breeds of dog and thankfully, where it is known, there is a simple DNA test which can be undertaken to find if a dog is a carrier of the relevant gene. Only one type of PRA is known within Entlebuchers and that is Progressive Rod-Cone Degeneration (prcd). It is an autosomal recessive gene, which means that for the condition to be expressed, the dog must inherit defective genes from both parents.

This is good news for breeding as it means that as long as one of the parents is clear of the condition then there is no risk of any of their puppies developing the condition.

When dogs are tested they are referred to as 'A', 'B', or 'C'. An 'A' is a dog who has two perfectly healthy copies of the gene and cannot pass the condition on to any pups. A dog classified as 'B' is a carrier of the condition, meaning that one copy of the gene is affected and thus gives a 50% chance of passing the damaged gene on to puppies. A dog classified as 'C' has copies of the gene which are both defective and will at some point in his life develop the condition. Usually, sight deteriorates from the age of three years onwards, but in some dogs it can be much earlier than this and may even be before the dog leaves puppyhood.

In all responsible breeding programmes a dog which is classified as 'B', and is therefore a carrier, should only ever be mated with a dog which is completely clear of the condition. In an ideal world, only dogs which are clear would breed and the defective genes would cease to occur within the breed, however with the very small gene pool of the Entlebucher population it would not be sensible to remove from the breeding programme dogs which are otherwise perfectly healthy, when careful control can ensure no future dogs are born affected.

In the natural world, a gene that is autosomal recessive would produce the condition in 25% of puppies and 50% of the breed would be carriers. Thankfully, since DNA testing for the condition has been the norm, in the modern generations of dogs from responsible breeders, I know of no dogs in our breed who have become blind through the condition.

Cataracts

The more I read about cataracts the more confused I become. There are a number of positions on the eye where cataracts may occur within the breed and more research is needed to fully understand the situation. Whilst some are hereditary in nature, it appears that diet and environment can also play a part.

The safest option would be not to breed from any dogs with cataracts, however in a very limited gene pool to rule out every last condition could lead to poorer breeding choices and greater risk of other problems developing. Some countries do choose to exclude all Entlebuchers with cataracts from the breeding programme, whilst others permit breeding from a dog with a 'single small cataract' in one eye, but only when bred to a dog who is clear. In the US a specific exception is made for Posterior Polar Cataracts where dogs with the condition are not excluded.

Although it is a matter of debate, cataracts do not often present a massive problem to the dog and in many cases where the cataracts are small they are barely noticeable to either dog or owner.

In many countries, the distance an owner has to travel to a Veterinary Ophthalmologist is considerable and eye-testing is sometimes arranged at Club events where there will be sufficient dogs present requiring the test, in order to justify the cost.

In the UK, the travel distance is exacerbated by the breed not being covered by the British Veterinary Association eye scheme. Instead, the test must be completed by a European College of Veterinary Ophthalmologists (ECVO) registered vet to ensure all parts of the test are recorded on the form rather than by a summary comment. Unfortunately, the number of ECVO registered specialists in the UK is very low.

Glaucoma

In simple terms, glaucoma is the build-up of fluid in the eye due to problems of drainage. High pressure in the eye can cause both headaches for the dog as well as pressure on the optic nerve leading to loss of vision and ultimately blindness. It can be a very painful condition and normally leads to the loss of the eye. Primary glaucoma can be hereditary. There is no definitive test which can show if a dog carries the gene(s) for the condition, partly because it is not a single condition. Progress is being made in this area with other breeds, but it may be some time before there is an easy test for all breeds. The best option is a gonioscopy, which is a painless eye test looking at the area at the front of the eye where fluid drains from the eye. A gonioscopy provides information that can be a strong indicator of the risk of developing the condition.

It is best not to breed from dogs which do have the primary form of glaucoma, but as it may not develop until after a dog begins breeding this is not always possible. It is another situation where having as much information regarding the background of parents and other family members is a valuable resource in evaluating the risk. This when combined with the information from the gonioscopy eye examination enables some level of prediction of the risk of any particular mating combination giving rise to puppies which might be affected.

Heart

As you will have realised from the previous section, health testing is an imprecise process and in taking a broad-brush approach, the danger is always that dogs are eliminated from breeding that do not have a hereditary form of a particular condition. However, with such a small gene pool it is a fine balance between putting the whole breed at risk and removing more dogs from the breeding programme than necessary. Heart murmurs fall very much into this category. Not all countries include a heart test prior to breeding. In Switzerland and in the UK a simple heart test is undertaken and dogs which show a heart murmur do not go on to breed. There can be reasons of the health and welfare of the breeding dog herself, not to use a bitch with a heart murmur for breeding, but the primary reason is to prevent genetic heart conditions from being passed on.

I know of a number of dogs in the breed who have heart problems. However, I do not know many who have the same condition. How closely the conditions are related is not my area of expertise, but I do look forward to a time when this can be assessed more effectively so we can be more discerning in our decisions as to whether to breed from affected dogs. Two of my own dogs have heart murmurs. Both are fairly low level. One has seen a heart specialist to identify the cause and there is no evidence of it being a genetic condition and nor should it affect her life. Wilma was declared to be very fit. However, she will not be used for breeding which may or may not be the right decision, but seems to be the safest approach for both her and future generations.

Hips

In common with many breeds, the Entlebucher can suffer from Hip Dysplasia. In general, in later life many animals have hip problems and the factors which affect this are four-fold. In testing breeding dogs, nothing can be done about problems caused by injury, over-exercise or inappropriate exercise at a young age, or diet. However, the element of hip problems which is genetic is something which can be reduced with good breeding.

Across the world, good breeders will have their breeding dogs x-rayed for hip dysplasia. This is normally done when the dog is around fifteen months of age. Before this, development of the joints is still taking place and it is therefore too early to identify issues. Testing at around fifteen months helps to ensure that the element that is recorded is less likely to be through injury or other problems.

The opinions on which dogs should then breed do vary, as does the scoring system in place in different parts of the world. In the UK each hip is scored on a points system, with the different parts of the hip joint being given a score separately for each of the left and right hip. A score of zero would be perfect in each hip. A score of 106 would be the very worst it could be, with a maximum of 53 for each hip.

The main FCI European grading matches to the UK scoring as follows:

A-1 - a total score of no more than 4 with a maximum of 3 on an individual hip.

A-2 - a score of 5 to 10 in total with no more than 6 on either hip.

B-1 - a score of 11 to 18 in total.

B-2 - a score of 19 to 25 in total.

C - a score of 26 to 35 in total.

D - a score of 36 to 50 in total.

E - a score of 51 - 106 in total.

Breeding from a dog whose hips are graded D or E would not be acceptable under the regulations of most countries. At the time of writing, no Entlebucher scored in the UK has received any worse than a B2 rating.

(See also note on timing of hip scoring of a bitch under the Luxating Patella section)

Ectopic Ureter

In very simple terms, ectopic ureter (EU) is a condition where the line (ureter) from each kidney to the bladder enters the bladder in the wrong place. There may also be times where the ureter runs some distance through the bladder wall giving rise to pressure preventing the normal passage of fluid. This is a complex condition and all this book can do is give a broad overview in layman's terms. There are others far better qualified than I to go into the more detailed explanations.

Pressure on the ureters can lead to urine backing up into the kidneys, ultimately causing death. One or both ureters entering the bladder below the sphincter muscles leads to incontinence. Not only is this inconvenient and very unpleasant but also gives rise to frequent bladder infections which can ultimately move on to the kidneys. There is no doubting that this is a condition to be avoided. In the Entlebucher breed, female puppies born with this condition are unlikely to survive early puppyhood, whilst male puppies are more able to find ways to compensate and it may not show itself until later in life. I am also led to believe that this is the reverse of the situation in some other breeds.

The condition is present in quite a wide range of breeds, however other than the Entlebucher and Appenzeller, very few are testing breeding dogs. The University of Zurich in Switzerland began researching the condition in both the Entlebucher and the Appenzeller some years ago in an attempt to develop a DNA test for the condition. Other universities in both America and now in the UK have also begun research, but it is thanks to Zurich that testing of our breeding dogs began.

Dogs are assessed through an ultrasound examination to identify the position in the bladder that the ureters enter. Those whose ureters correctly enter at the top of the bladder are graded 'A', an ideal situation. Those whose ureters enter further down the bladder are graded 'B', with a measurement of the distance from the bladder opening being recorded. Those whose ureters are positioned below the first valve of the bladder are graded 'C' and are regarded as affected whether or not they show any outward symptoms of the condition.

Around three-quarters of the Entlebucher population who have been tested are 'B'.

Over recent years, dogs which are affected have generally not been bred from, however there is a major discussion on whether removing them all from the gene pool is the right thing to do and without a clear picture of the pattern of inheritance it is hard to know the answer. What is clear is that parents who are not affected, even if both graded 'A', can give rise to a puppy with the condition. Having said that, the incidence of the condition has been reduced since restricting breeding to unaffected dogs.

The most recent research results from the University of Zurich suggest that the pattern of inheritance of EU is polygenic, that is there are multiple genes involved. There also seems to be a suggestion that the gene that gives rise to the majority of dogs being graded B, rather than the normal position A, may not be the same gene as the one that gives rise to an affected or 'C' graded dog.

The German Club (SSV) has focused heavily on having puppies from litters tested and since 2012 tested around half of all puppies bred there. What is interesting is that of the dogs tested bitches are twice as likely to be graded 'A' than dogs. In total those graded 'A' account for 10% of the total. 'B' is split fairly evenly between male and female and of the 8% of the population graded 'C' in the years 2009 to 2015 males accounted for 65% of those assessments.

Fatty Lumps (Lipoma)

These are benign lumps which can occur almost anywhere on the body. Particularly as a dog ages, they are not uncommon. They do not give rise to a problem in the dog, unless they occur in a location which impedes a joint. As lumps can have many other less benign causes it is always important to have them checked, but as it is not unusual for a dog who gets one to get many, this can be a difficult process involving many trips to the vet and difficulty in remembering exactly which have and have not been checked. A fine needle aspiration will enable the vet to look at the types of cells present and confirm they are of a fatty nature requiring no further investigation.

If you are the owner of a dog with multiple fatty lumps you will also soon get to know how the lumps feel just below the surface of the skin, moveable within a limited range and not apparently attached by any stalk to deeper tissues. They can grow quite large. Alfie has a very large mass on his shoulder which makes him look as though he needs to lose weight and gives an odd rolling gait on one side, but then he is twelve years old. There are also different types of fatty lump, so just as you think you have started to recognise what they are like, you find something completely different. Instead of an obvious lump they can also present as more of a flat panel of fatty tissue over a much wider area.

They can occur in places where they cause more discomfort, and one in Alfie's neck seems to make him swallow in a slightly more pronounced way at times. Shadow has developed a single fatty lump as she has got older necessitating a change to a different style of harness, as her old harness rubbed on a large egg shaped fatty lump on her chest.

Not all lumps are fatty ones, so don't get carried away assuming all is well if you do find a lump. It is far better to let your vet decide what is and is not worth worrying about.

Allergies

This may be indicative of the modern era, or it may be about the breed moving out of the land that has been its ancestral home and still adjusting to other surroundings, but Entlebuchers do show signs of allergies, much as their human families may do. This may be only certain breeding lines. I don't have enough information to judge. However, whether it is a rash on the tummy from grass pollen, or itchy eyes from dust mites, allergies are worth bearing in mind when trying to track down symptoms.

In the most extreme cases, allergies can lead to collapse and quick responses will be needed. On the whole, it is more about being on the alert if there are unexplained symptoms. Shadow is wheat intolerant, something I only discovered when one of her puppies alerted us to the problem. Once I changed Shadow's diet then problems of excessive wind, upset stomachs and random sickness all disappeared. I was only sorry I had not considered the possibility sooner.

Cruciate Ligament Tears

It is not uncommon for an Entlebucher to tear the Cranial Cruciate Ligament (similar to the Anterior Cruciate Ligament *ACL* in humans). Is it a genetic weakness? My answer is not scientific, but is based on observation. It is genetic in so far as the breed is predisposed to throwing themselves into every activity with an unsurpassed energy and enthusiasm, but there does not appear to be any familial pattern.

Any sportsperson will tell you that the more activity they engage in, the more likely it is that at some point they will sustain an injury. The same is true of our dogs. If you watch an Entlebucher jump, twist in the air, dart around spinning circles and generally taking advantage of whatever fun comes his way, you will realise that injuries will happen and, as with humans, some parts of their anatomy are more vulnerable than others.

Once an injury occurs, it is a difficult problem to manage, as asking an Entlebucher to remain calm and quiet for eight or more weeks is extremely challenging. Mind games and brain exercises can be invaluable to help use the dog's energy.

Back and Disc Problems

An Entlebucher Mountain Dog is long in the back. I realise that is stating the obvious, but it can hardly be a surprise on that basis that they will occasionally have back problems. It is no different to long-backed humans. There are things you can do to reduce risks, but much of it is down to the dog. If you have them carrying a pack, don't overfill it. Ensure they stay fit and trim and aren't carrying extra body weight. If possible, get them swimming regularly to ensure the muscles that support the bone structure are strong.

Equally important to the above is ensuring that any leg injury they sustain repairs properly and that the dog does not develop a gait which, while compensating for the leg problem / injury, puts unnecessary strain on the vertebrae of the back instead. This can lead to discs being damaged just as much in a dog as can happen in a human - and speaking as someone who has had a disc rupture, it is not to be recommended!

Luxating Patellar

Patellar Luxation is where the kneecap dislocates from the correct position. Although it can be injury related, as a condition it is more commonly a genetic abnormality. Whilst it is not common in the breed it would be normal for a breeding dog with the condition to be withdrawn from the breeding programme as a precautionary measure.

One point of note is that there is observational evidence to suggest that this problem could be exacerbated by muscle laxity in bitches approximately eight weeks post season, regardless of whether the bitch has been mated. As the dog's body follows a similar hormonal pattern regardless of pregnancy their body may go through some of the same preparatory processes for the birth connected with muscle operation. A bitch at this stage could therefore be more prone to both patellar luxation and other injury related conditions of the spine and rear hindquarters. This may also be a consideration when deciding when to have a bitch's hips tested.

Cryptorchidism

Cryptorchidism is a condition where a dog has either one or both testicles that do not descend. Technically it is regarded as being a problem if they have not descended by a year of age. In reality, it would be unusual to find one or both testicles that have not descended by about fifteen weeks of age going on to descend in the normal fashion, although there are cases where this does happen. I have known the condition in a number of dogs in the breed.

It does not seem to be an easy condition to prevent. As far as I understand, it requires a pair of defective genes, and therefore needs a faulty gene to be passed from both parents, in order for cryptorchidism to be expressed. Dogs who are known to have an undescended testicle are not allowed to breed. The problem is that, at the moment, whilst an affected dog is obvious, it is not clear if a bitch carries the gene until she produces affected puppies. Even then it is unclear if she carries one copy of the gene or is herself 'affected' having both genes defective, which of course will not show in any physical attribute in the female. Nor is it clear, by appearances, if an unaffected stud dog carries the gene.

Too little is known about the pattern of inheritance for any other measures, than removing affected males, to be taken to eliminate it. Until there is the clear ability to test for this gene it is more a case of trial and error.

Normally, a dog that has this problem should be castrated on health grounds, to prevent any risk of the undescended testicle(s) from becoming cancerous. There are specialist clinics where this can be done by laparoscopy which does speed the recovery process, although it can be a more expensive approach.

SHOWING YOUR DOG

Under the FCI categorisation of breeds the Entlebucher is included in 'Group 2 Pinscher and Schnauzer - Molossoid and Swiss Mountain and Cattledogs', based

Torfheide Bumble at Dolliesgang - Crufts 2014

on the origin of the dog being descended from the Molossus dogs. In the US the Entlebucher is included in the 'Herding Group' of dogs which seems appropriate as that is their primary function. Groupings in the UK differ to the US and here it is in the 'Working Group', as are the other Swiss breeds, as a result of their broader uses than simply herding and to align them with other dogs of Molossoid origin.

Showing is not a high priority in Switzerland, with the focus for the dog being on his suitability for herding and cart pulling and not solely on his appearance.

As a breed, an Entlebucher is not as well suited to showing as some other breeds due to his normal reticence towards strangers. Very few of our dogs are pleased to have a complete stranger examine them and the dogs are prone to not wanting to stand still while this happens. If you are going to show your dog, you need to give him as much experience as possible in being examined by strangers, to prepare him for handling by a judge, including being prepared to show his teeth. Many owners coming to showing for the first time find the reaction of the dog to being handled by an unknown judge can be quite an ordeal.

In the show ring, beauty is in the eye of the beholder and the conformation closest to the breed standard does not always win on the day. If a judge cannot properly examine the dog then, however good that dog may be, he is unlikely to do well. Training for the show ring can be a very important factor, not just in the initial examination of the dog but also when it comes to the dog's movement. It is hard for a judge to see the conformation of the dog in motion if the dog has his head to the floor as he trots around the ring.

It is as important for the handler to be trained as it is the dog. I have a beautiful picture of perfect movement from Wilma in the show ring at Crufts. I was not the handler! When I take her in the ring we trip over each other and rarely get a perfect trot. In the hands of an experienced handler, the sheer beauty of her movement was able to shine.

UK Showing

The UK Kennel Club is not a member of the FCI and, although it has a cooperation agreement with the international body, it manages its approach to both breed standards and showing in an independent manner. In the UK there is no automatic recognition of breeds which are already recognised by the FCI. Despite a breed already having an FCI breed standard (adopted from its country of origin), it has to be rewritten in the specific format required by the UK Kennel Club in order to be considered. It is only when the UK body accepts this standard that any classes open up to a dog in a pedigree show under Kennel Club rules.

Whilst the Bernese Mountain Dog has full recognition in the UK, the other three in the Swiss Mountain Dog family have been slower to gain acceptance. The Great Swiss has progressed furthest to date, whilst as yet the Appenzeller has no UK recognition by the Kennel Club.

The Entlebucher application to be included on the Import Register was accepted in 2006 but the dogs could not be shown at that stage as the breed standard had not been agreed. Once the breed had 20 dogs in the country, the Club applied for the next stage of recognition. This led to the UK Kennel Club agreeing the Interim Breed Standard for the breed to be effective from April 2013. This enabled the breed to be shown in any show under the Kennel Club rules which had classes for Working Group - Import Register.

Torfheide Beethoven at Skyeannroos (Basil), Norfolkfields Benji (Eiger), Alfie Bangwood (Buddy) (Photo Lizz Alexander)

The first Crufts dog show for which the breed qualified was March 2014, when three dogs, Torfheide Adrienne (Addie), Torfheide Beethoven at Skyeannroos (Basil) and Torfheide Bumble at Dolliesgang (Dickens) were eligible, although only the latter two were able to attend. They were joined in the ring by six dogs who had travelled from Russia for the occasion. As the classes were for Working Group Import Register they also included at that time the Beauceron and Great Swiss Mountain Dog breeds who, having been on the register longer and having more dogs in the country, were more heavily represented.

From April 2016, the Entlebucher was the only breed remaining on the Import Register in the Working Group in the UK. Consequently, although classes in shows remained few and far between, they did not include other breeds unless combined with other Groups, such as Pastoral. For Crufts 2017 there were seven UK dogs who qualified in addition to those travelling to the UK from France, Germany and Russia.

Pedigree dog shows under the UK Kennel Club generally have a 'catch all' class AVNSC (Any Variety Not Separately Classified) however despite the apparent wording this does not include those breeds still included on the Import Register. However, changes coming into effect in 2018 mean that all KC shows will

Torfheide Beethoven at Skyeannroos (Basil) – Crufts 2016 (Photo Lizz Alexander)

need to have a class for Import Register dogs and winners of Import Register Classes will now be able to progress through to the Group Stages.

USA Showing

As with the UK, the American Kennel Club (AKC) works independently of the FCI. The Entlebucher was first recognised by the AKC on January 1 2011 within the Herding Group and was first shown in the US based Westminster Dog Show in 2012.

Judge Training

Training judges to assess the exterior of the breed is important. Of most importance is ensuring judges for the breeding test are fully trained in all aspects of ensuring the dog meets the FCI breed standard. This is largely an objective assessment, although there may be some degree of opinion as to how certain

aspects of the dog are defined. For example, as with many things, whether the eye shape is almond or round, whether the ears are set high on the head or lower down, etc come in degrees rather than absolutes, which means a different box on the assessment form may be marked.

With such a small gene pool, focussing on correct conformation for the dog to be fit for its original purpose is significantly more important than any show ring assessment, in my opinion. Of course, showing a dog can be fun and I have rosettes to prove it, but one of the worst things that could happen to our breed is for subjective views on preferences for type to outweigh the core balance of the breed which is maintained through the Ankörung.

Even when training judges for the show ring in the UK, we focus on the FCI standard and the detail we look for in the breeding test. If a dog is good enough to receive an 'Excellent' or a 'Very Good' in the breeding test, then they should also do well if entered into shows. They are true to type and good examples of the breed and should be assessed as such by any judge worthy of the role. However, very few judges are trained in our breed in the UK and from reading critiques from the dogs that have been shown, some judges who are not specifically trained in the breed are unfamiliar with the detailed FCI standard. This can lead to assumptions based on the breeds they are more familiar with rather than the correct conformation of an Entlebucher.

The ratio of the proportions of an Entlebucher are not the same as many other breeds. Yes, they are long in the body compared to their height, they are meant to be (10 long to 8 high). Yes, they are broad chested, if they weren't then they would be of little value in pulling a cart.

There are also matters of preference which are neither right nor wrong. There are distinct body types in both the male and female dog. In the males there is both

Torfheide Beethoven at Skyeannroos (Basil) (Photo Lizz Alexander)

a slimmer and a broader build, whereas there are females with a more boxy appearance and others a little more rangy. As long as their proportions are correct and they are harmonious within those, then neither is right at the expense of the other. In breeding I am conscious not to go too far in either direction of the appearance, but to try to keep the types balanced within the breed.

Equally there are no precise requirements on exactly how much white a dog should have on his face or how broad the white on his chest should be. This is an area where tastes do come in to an extent and whilst the white should not be too 'flashy' one person's understated is another person's 'bling'! Only when it comes to the nape of the neck does the Standard specify a maximum size for any patch of white.

There are preferences as to the height and thereby the overall size of the dog. With the minimum height for a bitch being 42cm and the maximum height of a dog being 52cm (once the additional 2cm tolerance is taken into account) it gives broad scope for difference. However, focussing on one end of the spectrum or the other, does give rise to an increased risk of breeding dogs which fall outside of the acceptable range and should, if for no other reason, be avoided.

HISTORY

The Entlebucher Sennenhund, or Entlebucher Mountain Dog as he has become known in English, is believed to have descended from the now extinct Molossus Dogs of the Romans. These Mastiff type dogs were used by the Romans in war and left across those parts of Europe that were part of their empire. They developed across generations into different breeds serving various purposes according to the terrain and lifestyles of the area concerned. However, the regions in which the Swiss breeds originated did not have Roman roads and may not have been heavily populated as a result of the Roman passage. It is possible that these breeds derived from the Roman dogs only indirectly or from older stock with a similar origin.

Whilst being genetically close to a number of the mastiff breeds, the four closely related Swiss Mountain Dog breeds (Great Swiss, Bernese, Appenzeller and Entlebucher) have developed an appearance and character of their own. They were used as companions, guards and often to help manage livestock, a use they are still used in today. More in the male than the female dogs, the look of the mastiff can still be seen and in the UK it is not uncommon to be asked if the dog is a Rottweiler cross. Despite the frequency of people assuming an Entlebucher is a cross-breed, the breed has been recognised in its own right for more than 100 years.

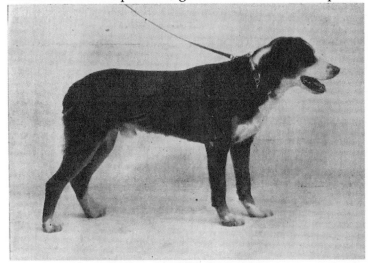

Poss v. d. Walke born 1926

Used by the Alpine herdsmen or 'Senner', the Swiss breeds are close cousins which developed originally in different regions of the country and which mainly take their modern names from those localities (Bern, Appenzell, Entlebuch). These were not always the names by which they were first known. Although their origin may be closely linked to the St Bernard, the latter was formally recognised as its own breed type as early as 1707 and was the first breed entered in the Swiss Stud Book. In comparison, the other four Swiss Mountain breeds continued in relative obscurity until the 1900s.

The need to use dogs for herding and carting reduced with increased mechanisation and their numbers declined in the 1800s. This also coincided with an influx of different breeds from other countries. However, thanks to a number of key individuals the four breeds were saved from disappearance and slowly developed to become the dogs we know today.

The Entlebucher Mountain Dog originated in the environs of the valley of Entlebuch, in the canton of Luzern, which neighbours Bern. As with his larger cousins, he was a farm dog, used for herding cows and pulling a small cart with a milk churn to the dairy. For a number of months of the year he would work closely with the herdsman in the mountains, giving rise to a bond between human and dog that is second to none. At home he would guard the farmstead and take care of the family.

The first written record of the Entlebucher was in 1889, when E Bauer from Aarburg described them much in the terms we would still recognise today with a height of between 40 and 50cms to the shoulder. Little further is known for the

Photo of the painting of Hotel Rothöhe on display in the current restaurant

following twenty years. However, shortly before the First World War, Franz

Schertenleib, a wine merchant from Burgdorf, came across the farm dogs when in search of the Great Swiss Mountain Dog. Schertenleib established Hotel Rothöhe and its surrounding wildlife park. Whilst the wildlife park was populated with

Entlebucher in 1915

considerable numbers of deer as well as llamas and monkeys, Schertenleib had a significant number of breeding Bernese Mountain Dogs. In visiting remote farms he encountered a large short haired dog which he took to an exhibition at Langenthal. He did not want the dog judged, but to obtain the opinion of the highly regarded Professor Albert Heim, a geologist but more importantly for our purposes a dog enthusiast. Heim who carried out much research into the Swiss breeds, declared the example to be a Great Swiss Mountain Dog and Schertenleib set about finding more examples. Professor Heim (1849 to 1937) had already begun to document the four distinct types within the Swiss Mountain Dog group in the early 1900s, but specimens of these dogs were not common. Schertenleib returned to Langenthal in 1913 with four smaller more agile dogs, with short coats and natural bob-tails which Professor Heim recorded as being of the type prevalent in the valley of Entlebuch. In 1914 Professor Heim wrote that those dogs had been found in Schärligbaches (Schärlig).

Trying to trace exactly which is the first named dog is difficult. The Swiss Stud book of 1917 lists the following:

Dogs:

7399 Arto vom Schlossgut (3/8/1913) (From Cäsar 6654 and Senta 6657)

7400 Blässi vom Schlossgut (14/2/1913) (From Bläss and Senta 6657)

7401 Caro (Gerber) (July 1913),

Bitches:

7402 Bläss (Zybach) around three years old and

7403 Grittli vom Schlossgut (17/3/1913) (From Bläss and Belline)

From this it is clear that Cäsar, Senta, Bläss and Belline predate 1913 but it is unclear on what dates any of these dogs were born. It also appears that Bläss was used as both a male and female name, which adds to the confusion.

What is apparent is that the intervention of World War 1 almost wiped out the breed and the process of establishing it needed to begin again.

After the war, it was Dr Kobler who set about developing the breed. At a show for the Swiss breeds in 1924 only the other three breeds were present. Thankfully, Schertenleib still had one possible breeding bitch, Babeli. In 1926 he found a dog

'Hess Tanner' near Brienz who sired a litter of five pups with Babeli. Babeli went on to have a second litter with Hess Tanner and then litters with Bäri, Spiro v Bruggen and Bär v Rotmonten.

It was following the first of these litters that, in a huge step of determination and faith, the Swiss Club (Schweizerischer Klub für Entlebucher Sennenhunde) was formed on 28th August 1926 in St Gallen. There were seven founder members. In addition to Franz Schertenleib and Dr Kobler there were, Paul Egger, F Kraner, Ernst Rüegg and Georg Scheitlin all from St Gallen and Willi Tobler from Thal.

The first Entlebucher show run by Dr Kobler, was held on 11 June 1927 in St. Gallen. It was attended by Professor Heim. There were sixteen dogs present, including another female which had been found on his farm visits by Schertenleib.

Babeli v. d. Rothöhe

In writing about the breed, Dr Kobler states that the foundation of the breed was around twenty dogs, and not more than twenty-five. However, whilst the original description gave the size as 'from 40cms', Dr Kobler in his writing stated a lower end of 36cms to the shoulder, although this was revised back to 40cms from the late 1920s. It can only be assumed that in re-establishing the breed the initial stock was a little smaller in the body, but that the original size was soon regained. This may explain where some of the modern misconceptions on the size of the dog originate, with some books still quoting the dog as being from the smaller size. There is also reference to the Entlebucher being a 'deerhound' rather than being mentioned in its traditional herding capacity. This may well go back to the early dogs being around Schertenleib's Hotel Rothöhe, which had many deer amongst its wildlife.

The first breed standard was agreed in 1927 and the fundamentals of the dog have changed little since that time. From then on, entries in the Swiss Stud books continued year by year. The breed grew slowly and is still the rarest of the four Swiss Mountain Dogs even in its native land.

THE AREA AROUND ENTLEBUCH

The Entlebuch valley is a UNESCO Biosphere Reserve. It is unspoiled and incredibly beautiful. It has a relatively low population and is one of the less wealthy parts of Switzerland. There can be nowhere more enjoyable to walk and appreciate the fresh air. The countryside is as gentle, yet magnificent as the dogs which take its name. Thankfully, whilst tourism is helping to sustain the area, the valley and surrounding countryside remain unblemished and with the protection that comes through its biosphere designation will hopefully remain so.

There are many ways that the dogs can be likened to the area. It is not glamorous or showy. It is not well-known and may never appeal to the masses. Instead it is understated with an effortless charm and a gentle aspect which is endearing to all who seek it out.

Elio v Schärlig (Photo Serge Renggli)

Foundation Dogs and Kennels

Following the breed standard being agreed, the first listing in the Swiss Stud Book of 1927 was number 27199 Babeli (v d Walke). Some of the markings were described, essentially black but with a white blaze, a white patch on the neck and four white paws. (The blaze being the white stripe running up the nose to the forehead). It also stated that she had a congenital bob-tail and that although she was born in 1924 her pedigree and breeder were unknown. She was bought from Schertenleib in Burgdorf and moved to Bruggen in St Gallen, which is why she was then known under the 'v. d. Walke' kennel name, rather than 'Rothöhe', which it is recorded as later. Interestingly, St Gallen is close to the border of the Appenzell region and away from the Entlebuch valley.

Also listed in that stud book were Gritli v. d. Rothöhe (f), and Blass v Innertal (m) born 1925 and 1926 respectively and both of unknown pedigree. The next listed was Bäri Hess (m) whose father is listed as Bärri Hess-Tanner and his mother as a bitch from F Schertenleib from Rothöhe bei Burgdorf (in what is now the Emmental region). Then follow two litters born to Babeli and Bärri Hess-Tanner, three puppies born in June 1926 and then a litter of eight in January 1927, both in St Gallen and carrying the 'v. d. Walke' kennel name.

Spiro born 1926

The remaining dog listed in that 1927 stud book was Spiro v. Bruggen (m) who again was of unknown pedigree, but his mother had been a 'Schertenleib' dog.

There were three photographs in that stud book, one of Poss v. d. Walke from Babeli and Bärri's first litter and two of Spiro. What is worthy of note is that the two dogs represent the different builds that can still be seen in the breed today. Poss was slim built and lithe, while Spiro was thick set and significantly broader. With both their heads and bodies in the relevant proportions, they would be clearly recognisable as the breed of today. With a database of all the Swiss Stud book records and those from other countries, it is possible to trace most of the breed through one or other of their lines back to Babeli. In the case of my own eldest dog that takes around thirteen or fourteen generations, depending on which line you follow.

Reading the listings of the very early dogs, most had a patch of white on the neck, some being listed as large patches. Overall, the markings noted in the early stud books were inconsistent, some having three white paws rather than all four, others having black on the chest, but in general the markings were much as we see today.

Tracking through those early dogs is not always easy. The initial dogs listed are of 'pedigree unknown'. After that, there is still confusion. For example on page 89 of the 1928 Swiss Stud Book Lorli v. d. Walke is listed as being the daughter of Bäri Hess-Tanner and Babeli v d Walke but on the following page her mother is listed as Gritli v. d. Rothöhe rather than Babeli.

1938 Pedigree of Gems v. d. Walke

It has become normal practice with Swiss breeders, and followed in some other countries, for a breeder's first litter to be given names starting with 'A', the second litter 'B' and so on. By this it is possible to know how many litters a breeder has been responsible for. It is interesting to track back when the pattern of using the same initial letter for the whole litter began. The Felsenzinne litter of 8 May 1931 were all given names beginning with

'B'. It is possible that this was breeder Rudolf Haller's second litter, but that is not clear. The first litter registered beginning all with the letter A was born in 1932 for breeder Walter Degen, a vet from Sissach, Switzerland. The first to continue the alphabetic pattern appears to have been the Echolinde kennel under Fritz Wegmüller, from Aarau, who had six litters from 1934 to 1959 A to H, missing out D.

The early kennel names were generally based on the location of the breeder. Many can still be found today in the names of roads, farms or small villages. Some have been immortalised on the sides of barns in the Entlebuch valley.

With so few generations back to the foundation dogs, it is inevitable that however low an inbreeding coefficient might appear when looked at over only five generations, it is significantly higher if looked at over a slightly longer period of time.

MAJOR SWISS KENNELS OVER THE YEARS

In more recent years there have been prolific kennels outside Switzerland, however here I will focus on the Swiss Kennels which have been fundamental to establishing the breed and to whom we all owe a debt of gratitude. Many Kennels throughout the history of the breed have had very few litters, often with only one breeding bitch over her reproductive lifetime. From the very early days Walke was the only breeder registering multiple litters, with 20 puppies over the 14 years from 1926 to 1940. Riedikon which started registrations in 1929 recorded 49 between then and 1947 and Marienthal 42 puppies from 1932 to 1950. The only Swiss kennels to exceed 100 puppies prior to the year 2000 were:

Beichlen with 112 between 1935 and 1972,
Hackenrüti with 106 between 1947 and 1966,
Nylackerberg with 180 between 1952 and 1998,
Steinegg with 158 between 1932 and 1989,
Stauffenfeld with 508 between 1963 and 1997,
Schurtannen with 118 between 1971 and 1996,
Glichenberg with 130 between 1973 and 2003,
Vorderrain with 114 between 1976 and 2000,
Stutz with 102 between 1978 and 1998,
Schnerlen with 121 between 1980 and 2002,
Chopfli with 135 between 1986 and 2003,

Hackenrüti Group Photo Luzern 1954

Other kennels have gone on to produce in excess of 100 dogs in more recent years, but only eleven Swiss Kennels had achieved that prior to 2000. Remarkable amongst them was the Stauffenfeld Kennel with in excess of 500 dogs, some of which themselves went on to be prolific stud dogs and which can be found across most pedigrees at some point. In going around the alphabet several times, they reused some names leading to much confusion in looking at family trees. There were for example three by the name of Sami usually referred to as Sami I, Sami II and Sami III Stauffenfeld respectively.

Priska and Urs Lötscher, Artus vom oberen Dorfberg (Photo Gina Graber)

Priska is wearing a real Entlebucher costume for high days and holidays, a 'Tschöplitracht', Urs a 'Chüjermutz', a festive, short jacket worn by the «Chüjer» (the mountain cowherds)

HISTORY OF THE SPREAD OF THE BREED

For a number of reasons, not least of which being two world wars, the breed was slow to spread out of its native Switzerland. Whilst most of the early development of the breed appears to have been to the neighbouring German speaking countries of Germany, and Austria, this did not happen to any significant extent for a number of years. However, one dog, Cibo von Haslenbach, was recorded in the Netherlands as early as 1939. The first recorded by the German Club (SSV) was not until 1952, although they may have entered the country earlier than this.

The movement of the dog into a wider geographic area did not happen until much more recently. For the most part, the spread only really took place from the 1980s. Dr Luescher, a Swiss national living in Canada approached the Canadian Kennel Club about registering dogs in 1985 and as that was not possible, began his

own North American registry for the dogs. The first to arrive in the Czech Republic was Delia vom Kornried in 1995. In the UK arrival was even later, with two dogs being brought over from France in 2002.

Of course, there are still many countries which have none of the breed, but through the migration of families, as well as the raised

Maja Kleinjenni with a more recent Kornried puppy
(Photo Sabine Mancosu)

awareness of this versatile breed, the spread is increasing. Even so, the worldwide population of Entlebuchers is still only a matter of the low thousands. Most countries have populations of under 500 dogs, with only small numbers breeding in most places. To ensure the strong and healthy development of the Entlebucher it is critical that breeding programmes look internationally to achieve the very best potential long-term results. It is equally important that countries try to work to the same standards and focus on common health issues to ensure that the breeding programme of any one country does not negatively impact the entire population.

Marco and Andrea Pisani in her Entlebucher Tracht, with Baika Susi v. Arvenstock
(Photo Sabine Mancosu)

FOUNDATION STOCK IN THE UK

Kenzo from Balihara Ranch, born in Slovakia in 2000 and Schweppes des Joyeuses Gambades (Chloe) born in France, were brought into the country by Lucy Denman in 2002. The pair had one litter of seven puppies in April 2003 and although none of their progeny went on to breed in the UK it was the first step for the Entlebucher in this country.

Queenie (Photo Serge Renggli)

Queen Viktoria Spod Hradze (Queenie)

Queenie was born on 4th September 2005 in Slovakia. She was imported to the UK in 2007 by her owner Kristina Fields and has gone on to become one of the matriarchs of the UK breed. She passed her Ankörung (breeding test) in Switzerland in April 2010 and then became the first bitch to breed under the UK Club. She has had three litters of puppies with a total of sixteen live births resulting. At the time of writing, three of her progeny have had litters of their own, and others are qualified to breed.

Queenie's first litter was with Leon von der Auenrüti from Switzerland. Her second was with Artus vom oberen Dorfberg, also from Switzerland. Her final litter was with Osiris von Thunstetten from Germany. Osiris is the half-brother of Shadow's (see below) father Nathan, which will mean progeny from this last litter from Queenie would not be able to mate with any of Shadow's puppies due to the closeness of the relationship.

Dogs from all three of Queenie's litters have qualified for the UK breeding programme, although in the case of the litter with Osiris it has so far not been possible to find a suitable breeding match within the UK.

At the time of writing Queenie is enjoying her retirement and at the age of twelve is living in Norfolk.

Aisha Princess of Beauty (Shadow)

Shadow, born on 6th February 2009, was the first British born bitch to have puppies in the UK. All of Shadow's mates have been Swiss. This is because she has one small cataract in one eye and would therefore not be allowed to breed in some countries. The cataract has not changed in size since she was first tested at two years old, but it has meant being selective with mates to ensure that the stud dogs

Shadow (Photo Sabine Mancosu)

chosen did not have any signs of cataracts. Shadow's first litter was with Rino von der Untergass. Unfortunately, none from this litter went on to breed. One who undertook her tests did have cataracts in both eyes, although of a different type to her mother's cataract. Others from the litter were tested and found to be clear.

Shadow's second litter was with Binto-Sämi vom Grundstiegeli. Torfheide Beethoven at Skyeannroos (Basil) from this litter went on to sire the first all-UK litter, but was then withdrawn from the breeding programme after his father, Sämi, developed glaucoma. Basil has since had a gonio test, which measures pressure on the eye and is the best indicator of a glaucoma risk. Despite it indicating that Basil may potentially be at risk, at five years of age he is showing no problems. Shadow's third litter was with Sämi's father, Falk vom Kornried. One from this litter has passed her breeding tests but has not yet had any litters of her own.

Shadow's final litter was with Max von der Auenrüti and from a litter of four pups three are hoping to breed.

Shadow is mother of 22 of the UK's dogs. Now at the age of nearly nine is enjoying her retirement in North Yorkshire.

These two bitches are between them the mothers of 37 and grandmothers to 21 of the dogs in the UK. Both are relatively small examples of the breed, but with careful choices of stud dogs, the next generation is larger. They have brought to the UK breed different characteristics. Queenie's progeny are more demanding of exercise, while Shadow's have a high proportion of tails curling too far.

CLUBS AROUND THE WORLD

Austria

Verein Für Schweizer Sennenhunde In Österreich (VSSÖ) - http://www.vssoe.at/
    The VSSÖ was founded in 1961 to represent the four Swiss Mountain Dog breeds. As with other Clubs around Europe that have responsibility for all the four breeds, the focus initially was on the Great Swiss and the Bernese Mountain Dogs. It was not until 1970 that the first Entlebucher litter was born under the Club.
    In order for an Entlebucher to breed under the VSSÖ they must have the following health tests. PRA, Cataract test and Gonioscopy, Hip Dysplasia and Ectopic Ureter. In addition to this, passing a breeding test (as described elsewhere in this book) is also a requirement, as is being placed in at least one show.

Belgium

Belgische   Klub   voor   Zwitserse Sennenhonden (BKZS)
 http://www.bkzs.net/
    The BKZS covers all four of the Swiss Mountain Dog breeds. The Club was formed in 1979. At present there is only one breeder breeding Entlebuchers under the Belgian Club Regulations.

Einstein van de Tiendenschuur (Alfie) (Photo Sonja van den Durpel)

Canada

The breed standard of the Canadian Kennel Club allows for a smaller dog than elsewhere, starting from just 40cm at the shoulder. Oddly the standard does not allow for a long tail, and whilst the dog is described as 'well proportioned in every way' there is no mention of the difference in proportions to the other Swiss Mountain Dog breeds. The breed is listed in the 'Working Group' as in the UK rather than the 'Herding Group' as in the US.
    The first Entlebucher imported into Canada was in 1986 by Dr Andrew

Luescher, from his native Switzerland. At that time the Canadian Kennel Club would not recognise the breed and Dr Luescher started a separate registry for the breed. That registry ran until 1995, during which time 80 dogs had been recorded. In the intervening period full recognition of the breed was obtained by Leslie Elliot of Tucker Kennels in 1989. The two separate registries meant that a number of dogs did not have official papers, complicating the foundation of the breed.

In 2000 NEMDA (See section on USA) was recognised by the Canadian Kennel Club as the official foreign breed club for the breed.

Czech Republic

Klub švýcarských salašnických psů http://www.kssp.cz

Litter H z Mokrovous - born 6.1.2016 – 2 months old – left to right Back - Ich. Auksis Interpola (maternal grandfather), Ich. Harry vom Saarnberg (father) Ich. Bea Annie z Mokrovous (mother), Ich. Esi Essi (maternal grandmother). Front - two boys and four girls. (Photo Pavel Pečenkovisee www.mokrovousy.cz/danka)

The first Entlebucher to arrive in the Czech Republic was Delia vom Kornried in 1995. Since then, with imports and careful breeding, the breed has grown to around 420 dogs in the country. No more than 3 litters per year were born in any year from 1998-2008. However, since 2009, the number of litters has started to rise significantly and in the last 5 years there have been about 20 litters annually.

Between 5-10 Entlebuchers per year are imported from abroad. This 'new blood' is extremely important for enrichment of the breeding base. The detailed statistics of development of the breed are available through the following link: http://www.kssp.cz/Chov/Menu/Plemenna-kniha.aspx (choose Entlebušský)

Where:

Počet vrhů = Number of litters

Počet štěňat = Number of puppies

Psů = Males

Fen = Females

The breeding kennels are listed: http://www.kssp.cz/Chov/Menu/Chovatelske-stanice.aspx (again choose Entlebušský)

Breeding dogs are tested for hip dysplasia, elbow dysplasia, progressive retinal atrophy, ectopic ureter and are also DNA tested. They may, as an option have their shoulders tested for dysplasia. They also undertake testing of character and conformation as part of their breeding assessment, at which point they must have an up to date cataract test and gonioscopy.

Entlebuchers are very versatile and Czech Entlebuchers are devoted to many sports. In some dog sports they are winning and passing the exams in the highest categories. Below is a summary of those sports in which the Entlebucher is involved in the Czech Republic.

Canicross

In canicross, the distances are about 5 km and thus more Entlebuchers are devoted to it compared to dogtrekking. Although some of them compete in the races, mostly they do it for fun.

Photo – Canicross: Kristynaphoto

Treibball

About 25 Entlebuchers regularly train in treibball and several of them compete and often win in the highest TRB 3 class at the races. Thanks to their enthusiasm and tenacity, they can compete with Border Collies, who dominate in this sport abroad. (see photo page 70)

Obedience

(This includes IPO - Internationale Prüfungs-Ordnung - line including obedience, track and defence, Czech national line and other derivations)

Entlebuchers are quite successful in this area. Some of them have passed IPO exams and national exams of different levels and they take part in, and often win, competitions. (see defence training photo page 63)

Agility

Several dogs and bitches train regularly in agility. As with Treibball, although their body is not shaped ideally for this sport, thanks to their enthusiasm and tenacity, they can compete with other breeds. Some of them compete in the A2 category (dogs in the L class and bitches in the M class). (see photo page 69)

Search and Rescue

Several Entlebuchers in the Czech Republic also do Search and Rescue (SAR) training and are very good at it. They usually specialise in 'area' or 'rubble' search and some have already passed Level 2 exams according to IRO (International Rescue Dog Organisation) rescue dog testing standards. (see photo page 71)

Dogbiatlon

Dogbiatlon is a new sport, but Entlebuchers are already represented here.

Photo – Dogbiathlon: Petra Haberzettlova

Dogtrekking

Dogtrekking is walking or running with a dog for a long distance (more than 80 km) and thus Entlebuchers are rather an exception here. However, one of them is the second vicemistr of Czech republic for years 2014 and 2015, the longest track he finished was 131 km.

Photo – Dogdancing: - Katerina Jozova

Photo – Dogtrekking: -Jiří Křivánek

Dogdancing

Dogdancing with wild and noisy Entlebuchers is a challenge. However, one of our Entlebuchers has passed successsfully the Master of Dogdancing 1 Exam.

Finland

Suomen Sveitsinpaimenkoirat - Finlands Sennenhundar ry
http://www.sennenkoirat.net/

The Finnish organisation is responsible for all four of the Swiss breeds. The first Entlebucher recorded in Finland was in 1958, but registration numbers in following years were low. The Club was founded in 1965 and has been recognised by the Finnish Kennel Club as the official breed organisation since 1972.

France

Association Française des Bouviers Suisses (AFBS) http://www.afbs-asso.com/

Although this club represents the four breeds, the Entlebucher presence is at present small. The first Entlebucher living in France moved there in 1988. Over the following nine years, with both litters born and imports, each year's registration figures still remained in single figures. It has only been since 2001 that the growth of the breed has been significantly more rapid, building year on year to 144 registrations in 2016. The current population of Entlebuchers in France remains a little below 1,000.

Those who are breeding through the Club are required to undertake health testing for hips and PRA as well as undertaking a character test and being placed in a show. However, not all those breeding in France are doing so under the Club. There are currently four breeders working to improve the health testing and quality of breeding in the Swiss Mountain Dogs. They are signatories to a quality charter. Of which the kennels 'Du Mystère des Bastides' and 'Des Elmiti' breed only the Entlebucher, having occasional litters and 'De Brapêche' and 'Des Cimes de Caras Galadhon' also breed the Great Swiss Mountain Dog. None are breeding in high numbers.

Germany

Schweizer Sennenhund-Verein für Deutschland e.V. (SSV) http://www.ssv-ev.de/

Covering all four of the Swiss mountain dog breeds, the SSV is the largest club for the Entlebucher in the world. The Club was founded in 1923, although the earliest Entlebucher recorded in the country was in 1951. Between then and 2005 more than 4500 Entlebuchers were born in Germany, the first litter having been in 1954.

The Club is heavily focussed on good breeding practices and protecting the health and welfare of the breeds it is responsible for. It is working at the forefront of developing and using breeding probability scores to manage common health conditions in the Entlebucher.

Health testing is undertaken for PRA, Cataract, Gonioscopy, Ectopic Ureter and Hip Dyslasia as well as the dogs undertaking an Ankörung. In addition to this, after the age of eighteen months they must be graded at least as very good in two shows.

Registrations in the last few years have been:

2014 - 404
2015 - 381
2016 - 406

Italy

Club Italiano Amatori Bovari Svizzeri (C.I.A.B.S.) http://www.ciabs.net/

Despite neighbouring with Switzerland, the Entlebucher is not well known in Italy. The Club was formed in 1988 with the initial interest being the Bernese Mountain Dog. Although there are now breeders of Entlebuchers in Italy, it remains a relatively unknown breed.

The Netherlands

De Nederlandse Vereniging voor Appenzeller, Entlebucher en Grote Zwitserse Sennenhonden (NVAEGZ) https://www.sennenweb.nl/NVAEGZ/sennenhonden/

Alwin van de Ursushoeve - NVAEGZ 40th Anniversary Show

History

The first Entlebucher in the Netherlands is believed to have been the Swiss dog Cibo von Haslenbach (born 31-12-1938), who arrived in 1939, but whose owner is unknown. There is then quite a gap before the next Entlebucher which is in the official Dutch Stud Book (NHSB), which is Zita v.d. Hündler (born 16-5-1961, CH-

108607) and the third was Dassy v. Neuweid (born 8-12-1958, CH-88943, NHSB-318977). Dassy was imported in 1963. Both dogs came from Switzerland.

Zita and Dassy went on to have the first litter born in the Netherlands in 1966 under the kennel name Groot Blankenburgh, owned by mister H.B.M. Gielen. He had been breeding Bernese Mountain Dogs since 1957. It was a small litter of only two pups, Onno and Olly.

Litters started to become more regular from around 1970, but there were still only one or two each year.

Numbers increased with further imports from Switzerland. Usually the imports were several pups from the same litter, for example Caro and Cara von Glichenberg, a dog and a bitch, in 1974, and Jsette and Jelka v. Gründelisbach in 1981.

Eleven pups in total were imported to the Netherlands from the kennel Glichenberg in the 1970s. Twelve puppies were also imported from the kennel Bois de Foyard, ten from Schädelmatt and twelve pups from Kornried. To this day imports to the Netherlands are continuing from the Kornried kennel.

Club

The first Dutch Club for all Swiss Mountain Dogs was founded in 1937: "De Nederlandse Sennenhonden Club". Partly due to the occurrence of the World War II this Club ceased to exist in 1947 after only ten years. However it was then reinstated in 1956.

As the Bernese Mountain Dogs were the more numerous breed, they decided to separate from the other three Swiss Mountain Dog breeds to have their own club. As a result, in 1975 the Club for the three shorthaired Swiss Mountain Dogs was founded: 'De Nederlandse Vereniging voor Appenzeller, Entlebucher en Grote Zwitserse Sennenhonden' (NVAEGZ).

NVAEGZ 40th Anniversary Show May 2015

In addition to this, from 1998 to 2012 there was a separate club only for the Entlebucher Mountain Dogs, 'De Entlebucher Sennenhonden Vereniging Nederland'. Now however only the NVAEGZ serves the interests of all three short-haired Swiss Mountain Dog breeds.

Under the NVAEGZ the tests which are compulsory for breeding dogs are: Hip

Dysplasia, Ectopic Ureter, PRA, Cataracts and Gonioscopy. Dogs also undertake the breeding test for both character and conformation to breed standard, as in Switzerland, Germany and the UK. In addition to this the dogs must be entered in at least one dog show.

Since the founding of the Entlebucher Mountain Dog Club of Great Britain there has been extensive contact between the two clubs.

Total Numbers
The estimated amount of Entlebuchers in the Netherlands is approximately 1100. However, the only large commercial breeders operate outside of the Club. Within the NVAEGZ those who are breeding from their dogs are all enthusiasts who have only a few litters to their names.

Norway

Klubben For Gårds- Og Fjellhunder www.kgfh.net

This is a club for both farm and mountain dogs and has a much wider remit

1st Norwegian Litter (Photo Lisbet Aarum)

than just the Entlebucher or even the Swiss breeds as a whole. However, the Club is principally based around showing rather than providing any detailed guidance on the individual breeds.

The first litter born in Norway was out of Ben v. Bergener Land and Kenmilfore Fleur(Becky)11 years ago, sadly they are all now gone, the last having died recently.

Poland

There is currently no club for the breed in Poland. The former club is no longer in existence.

Russia

In Russia the first officially registered Entlebucher dogs arrived in the Spring of 2004. Initially the male Xanthos from Balihara Ranch, (b. 27.03.04) was imported from Slovakia. He was described by judge Sonia Bellap Falletti, of Italy as being:

'A large dog with a strong bony structure. Very beautiful, well-bred head. Very good expression. Dark eyes. Full well-formed teeth. Scissor bite. Good ears. Good formation. Excellent, long, well-developed neck. Good croup. Good-sized body. Strongly lined upper body. Good angulation. Beautiful, free movement of the limbs. Long, upright tail. Outstanding temperament.'

Later that same year two bitches were imported from France: Vinny des Joyeuses Gambades (b. 09.04.2004) and Vanille des Joyeuses Gambades (b. 24.07.2004) Vanille was described by judge Katarina Schweitzer of Switzerland as 'A large, beautiful, well-formed bitch. Slightly lengthened nose. Good ears. Teeth normal. Good size. Strong formation. Good-sized body. Deep chest. Adequate angulation of the limbs. In movement the rear comes together a little. Very good hips. Top of the front legs parallel. Carries the tail well. Bright symmetrical markings. Excellent character.'

A second male dog Draco Brabusz (b. 16.06.04) was imported from Poland.

In the autumn of 2004, the dogs began to take part in shows and were of great interest to dog breeders. There were many people wanting to own Entlebuchers. As there was no immediate litter available, other dogs were imported from abroad. At the beginning of 2005, the number of Russian Entlebuchers rose by a further six as a result. Those dogs were: Kisme, Kaizer, Lorbas and Mauricio from Balihara Ranch, and Aqarelle and Aladdin des Joyeuses Gambades.

In the Autumn of 2005 the first Entlebucher puppies were born in Russia.

By 2007 the number of Entlebuchers had increased to 21 dogs, of which only eleven were born in Russia. By this time it was clear that although the first Entlebuchers were not at all bad and produced good offspring, new blood was needed to broaden the gene pool, so in 2007 Phobos from Balihara Ranch was imported. Phobos was described by judge Rita Michelin of Belgium as 'Medium proportions, strong enough, well-bred dog. Good formation. Good head, correct set of ears, charming expression. In motion a slightly soft back. Deep chest, good forechest. Excellent croup. Excellent angulation to the forelegs and hind quarters. Slightly open elbows. Parallel movements. Good temperament.'

Further imports were brought into the country in 2008; Sweet Sunny Szwajcar, Florisel vom Acholzli, Halla van het Bresserhof and Amareta Astra Interpola. Then in 2009 after much expectation two Belgian male dogs arrived Iago and Iaz van het Bresserhof.

At the World Championship Show in 2012 (Austria) the Best of Breed was Cazanova Iz Blagorodnogo Doma (owner O. Zabirokhuna), and Best Bitch Ewi Granitowy Pazur (owner S. Avseenko)

Since then, the population of Russian Entlebuchers has doubled. In that time, Russian dogs have repeatedly become World and European Champions and the breed has become increasingly popular.

Slovakia

Slovenský Klub Švajčiarskych Salašníckych Psov http://www.skssp.eu/
The Slovakian Club covers all four of the Swiss breeds. It was formed in 1992.
The only tests which are compulsory for breeding are hip dysplasia, elbow dysplasia and PRA. The dogs must also pass in two shows.

Sweden

Svenska Sennenhundklubben (SShK) http://www.sshk.a.se
The SShK covers all four of the breeds in the family, but as elsewhere the two larger breeds are much more numerous, with only the Bernese having annual registrations running into the hundreds, whereas it took the sixteen years from 2000 to 2015 for there to be 102 Entlebucher puppies registered.
Breeding dogs are tested for PRA, hip dysplasia and ectopic ureter. They must also undertake a breeding test and carry no other known genetic conditions.

Patrick Portmann with Binto-Sämi v. Grundstiegeli (Photo Sabine Mancosu)

Switzerland

Schweizerische Klub für Entlebucher Sennenhunde (SKES)
https://www.entlebuchersennenhunde.ch/
Much about the breed in Switzerland is covered throughout the book. Numbers of registered pedigree dogs are still very low in the country, with populations now being greater outside the breed's native land. Although there are between 100 and 130 puppies born in Switzerland each year, many of those are moving to other countries to live. In addition to the pedigree dogs, there are many farm dogs which are descended from Entlebuchers.
The Ankörung (breeding test) is run twice a year, in spring and autumn and follows the format described elsewhere. In addition to this the Club has other regular meetings, both formal and informal and also takes part in a number of the Festival Parades during the summer.
The Swiss Club whilst not the largest club, is the guardian of our breed and

especially with their work with the University of Zurich strives to safeguard the health and welfare of the breed as a whole.

United Kingdom

Entlebucher Mountain Dog Club of Great Britain (EMDCGB) http://entlebucher.co.uk/club/

The breed was first recognised on the Import Register by The Kennel Club in England in 2006. The UK club was formed in 2009 and received recognition by The Kennel Club at the start of 2011. The story of the Club is told throughout this book.

Southern Fun Day October 2013

United States of America

National Entlebucher Mountain Dog Association (NEMDA) http://nemda.org/

NEMDA was founded in 1998 and is the official breed club under the American Kennel Club (AKC). The basis of the Club began in 1996 when Rebecca Hahn, DVM, contacted known owners in the US. In the absence of full recognition by the AKC, the Club began its own registry and in 2000 presented their papers to the Canadian Kennel Club to receive recognition as an official foreign breed club.

In the short time to 2003 the Club had grown to have over 200 members and was recognised by the AKC as the official breed club in 2007.

The initial status of the breed allowed competition in companion shows only, but in 2009 this extended to Miscellaneous Classes and in 2011 to the full Herding Group recognition, with 2012 being the first year that the breed was shown in the prestigious Westminster Dog Show.

In order to breed in the USA dogs must have been health tested for the following and have results acceptable to the Club, hip dysplasia, cataracts (it is permitted for a dog with posterior polar cataracts or retinal folds to mate with a dog clear of those conditions) and PRA. A gonioscopy is recommended where offspring or siblings of the dog have developed glaucoma. A DNA profile of the dog is also required in the USA.

Import requirements

Import requirements vary considerably between countries. They can also vary within a country in consideration of where the dog is travelling from, with, in some cases, a clear distinction between rabies free zones and elsewhere. At the time of writing, the general rule, within the European Union and including Switzerland, is that a dog must be microchipped, have a Pet's Passport, have a current rabies vaccination and may then travel three weeks after that vaccination.

In terms of puppies, the earliest the rabies vaccination can be given is twelve weeks of age and therefore the earliest that a puppy can travel between countries is fifteen weeks of age. He will also need to be wormed between 24 and 120 hours prior to arrival in his new country.

An Entlebucher will bond very well with his new family at almost any age, however there are things which can be done to assist this. The provision of a comforter of some sort, which smells of the new family, is all the more important if the puppy is going to be slightly older before he joins his family and will help the puppy to 'know' and trust his new family, long before he moves to live with them. Where possible, visiting the puppy ahead of the move is also worthwhile.

To register the dog with the appropriate FCI recognised body in the country of import, the dog will need to have been issued with an export pedigree from his current country of registration. In the case of a puppy that will be his birth country.

It is always worth checking the requirements in detail before looking at importing or exporting a dog as it is not uncommon to find requirements that would be harder to second guess. For example, in Sweden in order to register and import a male dog, a 'testicle certificate' for the dog's father will be required, to confirm he has two normally descended testicles.

Also check out the costs of transportation. It is common to find, if you are using air travel, that on top of the charge by the airline there will also be airport handling charges at the arrival airport and possibly taxes as well. For the UK some of these can be avoided by collecting a puppy, imported from mainland Europe, by car.

APPENDICES

FCI BREED STANDARD

The first breed standard was approved in Switzerland in 1927 and accepted by the Fédération Cynologique Internationale (FCI) (the international body responsible for pedigree dogs in the majority of countries around the world) in July 1954. The standard is still owned by the Swiss Club (SKES) and was last updated in 2001.

Lex v. d. Auenrüti (Photo Serge Renggli)

Most countries work to the FCI breed standard for the breed. The only exceptions to this, as far as I am aware, are USA, Canada and UK. The UK standard which is currently an 'Interim' standard, as the breed is still on the Import Register, has been written to reflect the FCI standard as closely as possible but includes significantly less detail. As a result, as far as practically possible the Club in the UK works with the FCI standard to ensure uniformity of the breed.

The only standard which differs in any critical aspect is the American Kennel Club standard, which allows for a limit to height at the shoulder expressed in inches which is higher than in other countries, where the figure is expressed in centimetres. Other than that differences are minimal and generally reflect slight divergences in translation of language rather than of opinion.

The Entlebucher was historically a natural bob tailed breed, but years of careful breeding to reduce this trait mean that naturally bob tailed dogs are few and far between. Most countries no longer consider the bob tail as attractive and due to the regulations preventing the artificial docking of tails, a natural bob tail can cause confusion in both registration and the show ring. In the USA, some owners still favour the bob tail and there are lines which have succeeded in keeping that natural feature. However there are also other short-tailed Entlebuchers in the USA where the tail has been docked by the breeder, as docking is still permitted there.

Where docking takes place it becomes hard to tell whether the gene which causes the tail to curl further than normal in an Entlebucher is present or not, a trait which appears to be a hangover from the close relationship with Appenzeller.

FCI Standard

28.06.2002/EN FCI-Standard N°47 ENTLEBUCH CATTLE DOG
(Entlebucher Sennenhund)

TRANSLATION : Mrs. C. Seidler.
ORIGIN : Switzerland.
DATE OF PUBLICATION OF THE OFFICIAL VALID STANDARD : 28.11.2001.
UTILIZATION : Driving-, watch-, guard-, and farm dog. Today also a versatile
working and agreeable family dog.

FCI-CLASSIFICATION : Group 2 Pinscher and Schnauzer-Molossoid breeds-
Swiss Mountain and Cattle Dogs.
Section 3 Swiss Mountain and Cattle Dogs. Without working trial.

SHORT HISTORICAL SURVEY : The "Entlebucher" is the smallest of the four Swiss Mountain and Cattle Dogs. He originates from Entlebuch, a valley in the region of the Cantons Lucerne and Bern. The first description under the name "Entlibucherhund" dates from the year 1889, but for a considerable time after that date, no difference was made between Appenzell and Entlebuch Cattle Dogs.

Keyla v. d. Auenrüti (Photo Serge Renggli)

In the year 1913 four examples of this small herding dog with congenital bobtail were exhibited at the dog show in Langenthal and presented to Prof. Dr. Albert Heim, the great patron of the Swiss Mountain and Cattle Dog breeds. On account of the judges reports, they were entered into the Swiss Canine Stud Book (SHSB) as the fourth Mountain and Cattle Dog breed. However, the first standard was only completed in 1927. After August 28th 1926, the date of the foundation of the Swiss Club of Entlebuch Cattle Dogs initiated by Dr. B. Kobler, this breed was promoted and continued as purebred.

As the small number of entries into the SHSB (Swiss Stud Book) shows, the breed developed only slowly.

The Entlebuch Cattle Dog received renewed impetus when, apart from his hereditary qualities as a lively, tireless driving dog, his

outstanding suitability as a utility and companion dog was proved. Today, still on a modest scale, this attractive tricoloured dog has

found his admirers and enjoys increased popularity as a family dog.

GENERAL APPEARANCE :

Only just medium-sized, compactly built dog of slightly elongated shape. Tricolour like all the Swiss

Mountain and Cattle Dogs, very agile and deft; alert, clever and friendly facial expression.

Geri v. Trub (Photo Serge Renggli)

IMPORTANT PROPORTIONS :
• Ratio of height at withers to length of the body = 8 : 10.
• Ratio of length of muzzle to length of the skull = 9 : 10.

BEHAVIOUR / TEMPERAMENT : Lively, high-spirited, self-assured and fearless. Good-natured and devoted towards people familiar to him, slightly suspicious of strangers. Cannot be bribed as a watch dog. Cheerful and capable of learning.

HEAD : In harmonious proportion to the body, slightly wedge-shaped, clean. Head planes of muzzle and skull more or less parallel.
CRANIAL REGION : Skull : Rather flat, relatively broad, broadest between set-on of ears; slightly tapering towards muzzle. Occipital bone barely visible. Frontal furrow barely pronounced. Stop : Barely pronounced.
FACIAL REGION : Nose : Black, protruding slightly over front edge of lips.

Muzzle : Strong, well chiselled, clearly set off from forehead and cheeks, tapering evenly but not pointed. Slightly shorter than distance from stop to occipital protuberance. Bridge of nose straight.

Lips : Barely pronounced, close-fitting to jaw, with black pigmentation.

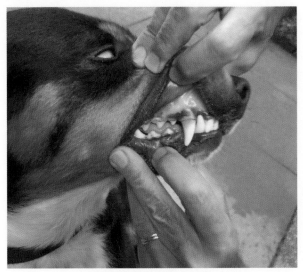

Photo Serge Renggli

Jaws/Teeth : Strong, regular and complete scissor bite. Even bite tolerated. Absence of one or two PM1 (premolar 1) tolerated. Absence of M3 (molar 3) not taken into consideration.

Cheeks : Barely pronounced.

Eyes : Rather small, roundish, dark brown to hazel. Expression lively, friendly, alert. Eyelids well fitting. Black pigmentation on rims.

Ears : Not too big. Set on high and relatively wide. Flaps pendulous, triangular, well rounded at tip. Firm, well developed ear-cartilage.

In repose lying flat and close to head; when alert, slightly raised at set-on and turned forward.

NECK : Of medium length, strong and clean, merging smoothly with the body.

BODY : Strong, slightly elongated.

Back : Straight, firm, broad, relatively long.

Loins : Strong, supple, not too short.

Croup : Sloping slightly, relatively long.

Chest : Broad, deep, reaching to the elbows. Pronounced forechest. Ribs moderately rounded. Ribcage extended, roundish-oval in diameter.

Lower line and Belly : Slight tuck up.

TAIL :

• Natural tail set on in continuation of the gently sloping croup.

• Congenital bobtail.

Natural long tail and bobtail equally acceptable.

LIMBS

FOREQUARTERS :

General appearance : Strongly muscled but not too heavy. Forelegs placed neither too wide nor too close together; forelegs short, sturdy, straight, parallel and placed well under the body.

Shoulders : Muscular, shoulder blade long, slanting and well attached to the body.

Upper arm : Length equal or slightly shorter than shoulder blade. Angle to shoulder blade about 110-120 degrees.

Elbows: Well attached to the body.

Forearm : Relatively short, straight, well boned, clean.

Pastern : Seen from the front in straight continuation of the forearm; seen from the side very slightly angulated. Relatively short.

HINDQUARTERS :

Luwa v. d. Auenrüti (Photo Serge Renggli)

General appearance : Well muscled. Seen from behind hind legs not too close together, straight and parallel.

Upper thigh : Fairly long. Forming a rather wide angle with the lower thigh at the stifle joint. Thighs broad and strong.

Lower thigh : Approximately equal length to upper thigh, clean.

Hock joint : Strong, set relatively low, well angulated.

Hock : Fairly short, sturdy, vertical and parallel in position.

Dewclaws must be removed, except in those countries where the removal is prohibited by law.

FEET : Roundish, with tight, well arched toes, pointing straight forward. Nails short and strong. Pads coarse and robust.

GAIT / MOVEMENT : Ground covering, free, easy movement with strong drive from rear. Seen from front or rear, legs track in a straight line.

COAT

HAIR : Double coat (Stockhaar). Topcoat short, close fitting, harsh and shiny. Undercoat dense. Slightly wavy hair on withers and/or back tolerated, but not desirable.

COLOUR AND MARKINGS : Typically tricolour. Basic colour black with "yellow-to reddish-brown" tan markings which should be as symmetric as possible.

The tan markings are placed above the eyes, on cheeks, on muzzle and throat, on either side of chest and on all four legs. On the legs the tan markings are situated between the black and the white.

Undercoat dark grey to brownish.

White markings :

• Distinct small with blaze which runs without interruption from top of the head over the bridge of nose and can wholly or partially cover the muzzle.

- White from chin over throat without interruption to chest.

- White on all four feet.

- On a long tail white tip desirable.

Undesirable but tolerated : small white patch on nape of neck (not more than half the size of a palm).

HEIGHT :

Height at withers : Dogs 44-50 cm, tolerance up to 52 cm. Bitches 42-48 cm, tolerance up to 50 cm.

Timber-Basco v. Simonhof (Photo Serge Renggli)

FAULTS : Any departure from the foregoing points should be considered a fault and the seriousness with which the fault should be regarded should be in exact proportion to its degree and its effect upon the health and welfare of the dog.

- Lack of typical sex-specific appearance.
- Distinctly unbalanced.
- Bone too coarse or too fine.
- Insufficient musculature.
- Round skull.
- Stop too defined.
- Muzzle short, too long or snippy; nasal bridge not straight.
- Mouth very slightly undershot.
- Absence of teeth other than 2 PM1 (premolars 1).
- Eyes too light, too sunken or protruding.
- Eyelids slightly slack.
- Ears too deep-set, too small or too pointed, carried standing off or folded.
- Back too short, swayback or roach back.
- Croup overbuilt or falling away.
- Chest too flat-ribbed or barrel-shaped, lacking in forechest.
- Kinky tail; tail carried over back.
- Forequarters not sufficiently angulated.
- Forelegs turned out or crooked.
- Pastern weak, or down on pastern.

• Hindquarters not sufficiently angulated, cow-hocked or bandy legs, close behind.

• Feet longish, spread toes.

• Movement : short stride, stilted, close coming and going, weaving.

• Faults in marking :

- Interrupted blaze.

- White patch on nape of neck bigger than half of a palm.

- White distinctly reaching above pasterns ("boots").

- White not on all 4 feet.

- White collar around the whole neck (serious fault).

- Divided white on chest (serious fault).

- Forelegs : absence of tan between the white and the black (serious fault).

- Absence of any white on head = totally black head (very serious fault).

• Unsure behaviour, absence of liveliness, slight sharpness.

QUALIFYING FAULTS :

• Aggressive or overly shy dogs.

• Any dog clearly showing physical of behavioural abnormalities shall be disqualified.

• Overshot, distinctly undershot or wry mouth.

• Entropion, ectropion.

• Yellow hawk eyes, wall eyes, blue eyes.

• Ring tail.

• Coat too long, soft (no double coat).

• Faults in colour :

- Other than tricoloured coat.

- Basic colour other than black.

• Undersize, oversize regarding tolerances.

N.B.:

• Male animals should have two apparently normal testicles fully descended into the scrotum.

• Only functionally and clinically healthy dogs, with breed typical conformation should be used for breeding.

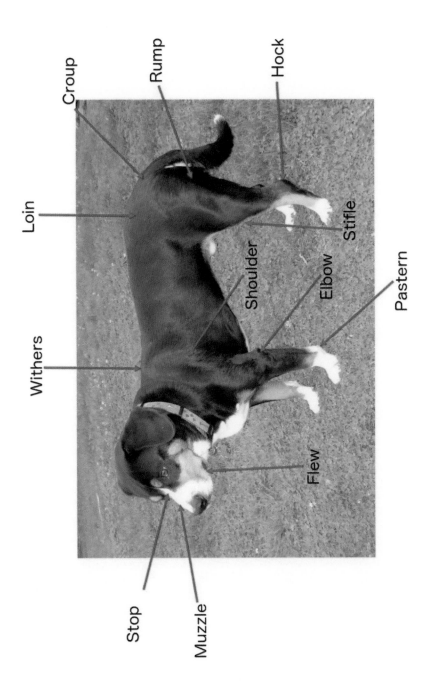

Alfie illustrating some of the key parts of a dog

UK BREED STANDARD

Interim Breed Standard Agreed by the EMDCGB with the UK Kennel Club effective from 1st April 2013

General Appearance
Tri coloured. Medium sized Swiss herding dog. Solidly built, longer than high.

Characteristics
Agile, alert, clever, high spirited.

Temperament
Self assured and fearless. Good natured, devoted to family but may be slightly suspicious of strangers.

Head and Skull
Head in proportion to body, clean and slightly wedge shaped. Length of muzzle slightly shorter than length of skull. Planes of muzzle and skull almost parallel. Skull flat, broadest between ears, tapering gently towards the muzzle. Slight furrow and stop without prominent occiput. Lips close fitting with black pigmentation. Prominent, black nose.

Valeria v. Rickental (Photo Serge Renggli)

Eyes
Medium sized, round, dark brown to hazel, well fitting eyelids, eye rims black, lively expression.

Ears
Set on high. Medium sized, pendulous, triangular in shape, relatively wide at base, well rounded at tip. Lying flat in repose. When alert slightly raised and brought forward.

Mouth
Jaws strong with a perfect, regular and complete scissor bite. Level bite

tolerated.

Neck

Moderate length, muscular, strong and clean, merging smoothly into shoulders.

Forequarters

Shoulders long, strong, sloping and well muscled, forming a distinct angle with upper arm which appears approximately equal in length to shoulder. Elbows set close to body and positioned vertically below withers. Forearm well boned, straight when viewed from all sides. Slight slope to relatively short pastern.

Shiva v. d. Untergass (Photo Serge Renggli)

Body

Length from point of shoulder to point of buttock slightly greater than height at withers. Forechest well developed. Broad, oval chest, well sprung ribs with brisket reaching at least to the elbow, with slight tuck up to underline. Back strong, level with broad, well muscled loin.

Hindquarters

Croup long, broad and gently sloping. Well developed first and second thigh with moderate bend of stifle. Hock joint strong and distinctly angulated. Hocks well let down. Viewed from behind, legs not too close together, straight and parallel.

Feet

Round and compact with well arched toes, turning neither in nor out. Pads thick and strong.

Tail

Set on of tail follows the line of the gently sloping croup, or natural bobtail, both equally acceptable, hanging straight down when at rest, never kinked. In motion or when alert can be elevated but not curled over the back. Ring tail highly undesirable.

Gait/Movement
Free, easy movement with good drive from the hindquarters.

Coat
Double coated. Topcoat short, close fitting, harsh and shiny, dense undercoat. Slight wavy hair on withers and/or back tolerated but not desirable.

Colour
Tricolour, predominant colour black, with symmetrical tan markings and clean white markings.

Tan markings: above the eyes, on cheeks, muzzle, throat, either side of chest and on all four legs. Tan markings on the legs are between the black and the white.

Nathan v. Thunstetten (Photo Grete Stadlbauer)

White markings: a distinct blaze which runs without break from top of head over bridge of nose, wholly or partially covering muzzle from under jaw to chest. White on all four feet. On full length tail a white tip is desirable. Small white patch on nape of neck is undesirable but tolerated.

Size
Ideal height at withers Dogs 44-50cms (17 ½ - 19 ¾ ins); Bitches 42-48cms (16 ½ - 19 ins). An upper size tolerance of 2cms (¾ in) acceptable.

Faults
Any departure from the foregoing points should be considered a fault and the seriousness with which the fault should be regarded should be in exact proportion to its degree and its effect upon the health and welfare of the dog and on the dog's ability to perform its traditional work.

Note
Male animals should have two apparently normal testicles fully descended into the scrotum.

ENTLEBUCHER MOUNTAIN DOG CHARACTER TEST

The test of character is one of the sections of the Ankörung but can also be used on a stand-alone basis to assess the suitability of the dog for other roles.

The character test is designed to cover all aspects of character and while some of the situations included may seem artificial, they are designed to cover a range of unpredictable situations which the dog and owner may encounter.

The test is broken into four parts. Exercises are generally performed off lead, although some countries work on-lead.

1) The candidate is asked a number of questions about the dog's situation and the type of environment in which he lives. They are also asked what in their opinion makes the dog special.

2) The first part of the main test assesses the following:
   a) How the dog reacts in a crowd of people.
      i) The dog and owner weave in and out of a crowd of people
      ii) The dog and owner stand in the middle of a circle of people –
         (1) The people advance slowly towards the dog and owner and then retreat.
         (2) The people advance rapidly towards the dog and owner and then retreat.
         (3) The circle of people clap
      iii) The dog is surrounded by a small crowd of people and held on a lead while the owner goes out of sight. The dog is then released to find his owner.

The dog is held while the owner walks away

   b) The dog at play:
      i) The owner plays with the dog without any toys.
      ii) The owner plays with the dog with a toy
      iii) The assessor plays with the dog with a toy.

3) Part two of the main test looks at how the dog reacts to strange noises and visual and other sensory stimuli.
   a) The dog and owner walk across tarpaulins spread out on the ground

b) The owner and dog walk up and down a line marked on the grass with the dog at heel

c) They then walk up and down with people passing

d) As they walk up and down a horn is sounded

e) As they walk up and down a. bell is rung

The owner walks with the dog close by

f) As they walk up and down someone drags a line of tin cans along the ground

g) They walk up and down with the distraction of cordon tape attached to a stick being waved on the ground in front of them

h) They walk up and down with the distraction of a waffle board being waved to make a noise

i) They walk up and down with an umbrella being opened and closed towards them

j) As they walk a balloon is deflated next to them

k) As they walk a canister filled with stones is dragged along the ground next to them

l) As they walk two planks of wood are clapped together

m) They walk up to a sheet being held up across their path. The sheet is then dropped to the ground and they walk across it. The exercise is repeated a second time.

4) Part three of the test looks at how the dog handles being approached by someone greeting the dog's owner and when around another dog on a lead. This part of the test is on lead.

   a) The owner sits with the dog while someone approaches to talk to them

   b) The owner sits with the dog while someone with a dog passes

   c) The owner stands with the dog while someone with a dog passes

   d) The dog's lead is tied to a stake while the owner hides out of the way

   e) A person approaches and walks around the dog at a reasonable distance

      i) A person with a dog walks around the dog at a reasonable distance

      ii) The person (without the dog) goes up and fusses the dog.

DETAILED HISTORY OF THE UK POPULATION

The following shows the overall development of the UK population. The figure in brackets after the year is the number of dogs in the UK at the end of that year. If trying to compare these to numbers registered with the Kennel Club, it should be noted that not all dogs have been registered.

2002 - (2) Kenzo from Balihara Ranch and Schweppes des Joyeuses Gambades (Chloe) were the first two Entlebuchers in the UK.

2003 - (6) Seven puppies were born to Kenzo and Chloe - one of which moved to Ireland and one to Norway. Chloe also moved to Norway.

2004 - 2006 - (9) Three dogs moved to the UK, Guapo from USA, Eika from Switzerland and Marbella from Balihara Ranch from Slovakia. Only Marbella was registered.

2007 - (10) Queen Viktoria Spod Hradze (Queenie) moved to the UK from Slovakia.

2008 - (11) Einstein Van de Tiendenschuur (Alfie) moved to the UK from Belgium and Orson from Balihara Ranch moved to the UK from Slovakia. Marbella, whose story is told elsewhere in this book, was tragically killed on a railway at the age of three.

Queen Viktoria Spod Hradze (Queenie) 2009

2009 - (16) Akai d'Hos Moinhos d'Alvura, originally a Portuguese dog, moved to the UK from Austria for the purpose of having her litter in the UK. She gave birth to four puppies including Aisha Princess of Beauty (Shadow). In addition to this a dog was registered with the Kennel Club that the Club has not managed to track down.

2010 - (22) An unregistered dog moved from Germany to the UK and Victory Megan vom Kornried was imported from Switzerland with the intention of her joining the breeding programme. Sadly, as told elsewhere in this book she was unable to have puppies. In that year, on 27th September the first litter under the UK Club was born to Queenie. She had five live puppies including Annie and Aida who both went on to join the breeding programme. Eika moved back to Switzerland in that year.

2011 - (26) Shadow had her first litter this year with seven live pups. However, in the same year two of Shadow's brothers moved to Germany and one later died following a viral infection. Sadly, it was also the year in which Kenzo (one of the first of the breed in the UK) died at the age of eleven years and three months of age.

2012 - (37) Both Queenie and Shadow went on to have their second litters. Queenie had six pups and Shadow five.

2013 - (49) Queenie had her final litter with five pups and Shadow had a litter of six pups this year. There were two imports one from Slovakia and one Bilbo vom Coesfelder Hügli brought in from Germany to help broaden the gene pool.

Norfolkfields Bella (Photo Sarah Fulker)

In that year we sadly lost Guapo at the age of just over twelve and a half.

2014 - (51) There was only one litter born in the UK in 2014, that was to Annie Swiss Dawn, a daughter from Queenie's first litter. Annie had four pups. There were also two imports, one from the Czech Republic and one from Switzerland. However, in that year three of the original 2003 litter died. Also in 2014 Megan moved to live in Germany.

2015 - (69) This was a big year for the breed in the UK. There were two litters born. Shadow had her fourth and final litter of four pups. Bella Norfolkfields, a bitch from Queenie's second litter, had her first litter of seven pups. There were also nine dogs imported during the year, coming from Russia, Czech Republic, Italy and Switzerland. Another from the 2003 litter died in this year and it is assumed by this stage the one pup we were not in contact with from that litter had also died.

2016 - (78) The first all UK mating took place in this year between Aida

Norfolkfields, from Queenie's A litter and Beethoven Torfheide at Skyeannroos (Basil) from Shadow's B litter. There were three live pups in the litter. There were also six imports, one from Poland and five from Switzerland.

2017 - (92) At the time of writing, the number of the breed in the UK is 92. Bella Norfolkfields had a second litter of seven pups, including one named Babeli, after one of the original Swiss breeding bitches, and who will hopefully join the UK breeding programme. In addition to this, eight imports have arrived into the country, a number of whom have been brought in with the specific intention of broadening the breeding programme. Sadly, we also had the first loss of the new generation of dogs born in the UK, when Norfolkfields Ashdon died following a car accident.

The UK population is still relatively young with the upper age currently being twelve years old. We hope to reach the 100 mark during 2018 and with three imports already planned we are well on the way to our target.

Breed Stand at Discover Dogs Crufts 2017

BREEDING TEST CONFORMATION ASSESSMENT FORM

Entlebucher Mountain Dog Club of Great Britain
CONFORMATION ASSESSMENT

Registered Name: _____	☐ Male	☐ Female
DOB: _____ KC Number: _____	Phone: _____	
Breeder: _____ HD left: _____ right: _____	Size: _____	
Owner: _____	Testicles descended: ☐	
Address: _____	PRA: _____	

GENERAL APPEARANCE

1. Type: ☐ too light ☐ light ☐ medium ☑ compact/sturdy ☐ rough ☐ heavy ☐ plump

2. Bones: ☐ too light ☐ medium ☑ sturdy ☐ heavy ☐ too heavy

3. Body: ☐ too short ☐ short ☑ typical ☐ long ☐ too long

HEAD

4. Head: ☐ too small ☐ narrow ☐ delicate ☑ typical ☐ broad ☐ massive

5. Top of Head: ☐ too flat ☑ flat ☐ slightly domed ☐ strongly domed

6. Stop: ☐ too flat ☐ slight ☑ correct ☐ steep

7. Muzzle: ☐ too short ☐ short ☑ normal ☐ long

8. Width of Muzzle: ☐ pointed ☐ narrow ☑ typical ☐ wide

9. Flews: ☐ open ☐ slightly open ☑ closed

10. Bite: ☐ over ☐ under ☐ even ☐ barely scissored ☑ strong, regular scissor ☐ irregular scissor

11. Missing Teeth _____

12. Teeth: ☐ weak ☐ medium ☑ strong ☐ very strong

13. Eye shape: ☐ small ☐ almond-shaped ☐ deep-set ☑ round ☐ big ☐ protruding

14. Eye colour: ☐ too light ☐ light ☐ brown ☑ dark brown

15. Eyelid: ☐ tight ☑ well-fitting ☐ open

16. Ear Position: ☐ too low ☐ low ☑ typical ☐ high ☐ too high

17. Ear Posture: ☐ open ☐ lying back ☑ typical

18. Ear Shape: ☐ too small ☐ pointed ☐ folded ☑ correct

19. Throat: ☐ dewlap ☐ tight ☐ not typically connected ☑ harmoniously connected

BODY

20. Chest: ☐ narrow ☐ slightly deep ☐ not fully formed ☑ typical ☐ too round

21. Shoulders: ☐ loose ☐ slightly loose ☑ correct

22. Elbows: ☐ strongly turned outward ☐ turned outward ☑ correct ☐ turned inward ☐ strongly turned inward

23. Lower Line: ☐ too tucked up ☐ tucked up ☑ slightly tucked up/ideal

24. Back: ☐ sway back ☐ slightly soft ☐ soft ☑ sturdy/level ☐ slightly humped ☐ humped

25. Croup: ☐ too sloping ☐ sloping ☑ normal ☐ flat ☐ very short and flat

26. Tail: ☐ congenital bobtail ☐ docked ☐ long

27. Tail set: ☐ high ☐ high arc ☑ normal

28. Tail abnormality: ☐ kinked ☐ hooked ☐ ring ☐ other abnormality ☑ No abnormality

FOREQUARTERS

29. Front legs: ☐ turned outward ☐ slightly turned outward ☑ straight ☐ slightly turned inward ☐ turned inward

30. Front Pasterns: ☐ yielding ☐ soft ☐ slightly soft ☑ normal ☐ steep

31. Front Angulation: ☐ steep ☐ slightly angulated ☑ distinct/ideal ☐ too strong/over angulated

32. Paws: ☐ rabbit ☐ slightly flat ☑ normal ☐ slightly splayed ☐ splayed

REARQUARTERS

33. Back Legs: ☐ cow hocked ☐ turned outward ☐ slightly turned outward ☑ correct ☐ turned inward ☐ bow-legged

34. Rear Pasterns: ☐ yielding ☐ soft ☐ slightly soft ☑ normal ☐ steep

35. Rear Angulation: ☐ steep ☐ slightly angulated ☑ distinct/ideal ☐ too strong/over angulated

MOVEMENT/COLOUR

36. Gait: ☐ inhibited ☐ slightly inhibited ☐ adequately free ☑ free/striding ☐ overstepping

37. Movement error: ☐ shoulder turned in ☐ shoulder turned out ☐ front legs lacing as moves ☐ Hip turned in ☐ hip turned out ☐ rear legs lacing as moves ☑ No fault

38. Pigmentation: ☐ incomplete ☐ adequate ☑ complete (black)

39. Coat: ☐ long ☐ slightly long ☑ short double coat (Stockhaar) ☐ abundant brown undercoat ☐ slight brown undercoat ☑ no brown undercoat

40. Tan Marking: ☐ too light ☐ light ☑ dark ☐ sooty

41. White Marking: ☐ very little ☐ not enough ☑ typical ☐ abundant ☐ over abundant

42. Colour Distribution: ☐ strongly asymmetric ☐ slightly asymmetric ☑ conforms to standard ☐ nape patch ☐ boots

General Impression unsatisfactory:	☐ satisfactory	☐ good	☑ very good	☑ excellent
Character Assessment:	☑ passed	☐ deferred	☐ failed	(c.f. character assessment for information)

Approved for Breeding:	☐ Yes	☐ Deferred	☐ No
Comments: _____			

Date: _____ Evaluators: _____

Valid until - _____ Renewed until - _____

Included by permission of the EMDCGB and based on the original SKES form

BREEDING TEST CHARACTER ASSESMENT FORM

 Entlebucher Mountain Dog Club of Great Britain
CHARACTER ASSESSMENT

Registered Name: _____	☐ Male ☐ Female
DOB: _____ Age in months: _____	KC Number: _____
Owner: _____	Phone: _____
Address : _____	

Character assessment: ☐ First Assessment	☐ Second Assessment	☐ Recall	☐ Deferred
Dog handler: ☐ Primary	☐ Representative	☐ Breeder	☐ Other: _____
Living arrangements: ☐ Rural	☐ Remote	☐ Rarely around traffic	☐ Only dog in the household
☐ City	☐ Busy	☐ Often around traffic	☐ Other dogs, animals, children
Contact to strangers: ☐ Often	☐ Rarely		**Owners:** ☐ 1 ☐ 2 ☐ 3

Special characteristic: _____

Healthy: ☐ Yes ☐ No   **Medication:** _____

Accidents: ☐ No ☐ Yes: _____	**In season:** ☐ Yes ☐ No

Training: ☐ None ☐ Puppy Class ☐ Obedience Class ☐ Sports Dog ☐ Family Dog ☐ Hunting Dog

Behaviour towards handler and strangers	Good	OK			
Free roam with master/mistress	☐	☐ Bond intact	☐ Sticks	☐ Loose bond
Master/Mistress walks with dog through group	☐	☐ Normal	☐ Reluctant	☐ Nervous
Groups approaches dog	☐	☐ Sociable	☐ Reluctant	☐ Nervous
Playing with master/mistress without toy	☐	☐ Normal	☐ Unfamiliar	☐ Passive
Playing with master/mistress with toy	☐	☐ Takes Toy	☐ Plays	☐ Passive
Playing with strangers/evaluator	☐	☐ Takes Toy	☐ Disinterested	☐ Backs away
Group/circle closes in around dog and master/mistress (opening and closing slowly)	☐	☐ Normal	☐ Unsettled	☐ Nervous
(Opening and closing quickly)	☐	☐ Normal	☐ Unsettled	☐ Nervous
Dog leaves circle and goes to master/mistress	☐	☐ Active	☐ Hesitant	☐ Nervous
Exposure to optical distraction (bandana, plastic strip, umbrella, etc.)	☐	☐ Normal	☐ Unsettled	☐ Jumpy
Exposure to aural distraction (canister with stones, horn, bell, clanging metal, crumpling plastic bag etc.)	☐	☐ Normal	☐ Unsettled	☐ Jumpy

ASSESSMENT

Behaviour towards strangers
☐ Fearless ☐ Cautious ☐ Serious ☐ Indifferent ☐ Moves Away ☐ Passive ☐ Other: _____

Behaviour towards other dogs
☐ Fearless ☐ Cautious ☐ Serious ☐ Indifferent ☐ Nervous ☐ Passive ☐ Other: _____

CONCLUSION

Positive: ☐ Active ☐ Attentive Focussed Confident ☐ Sociable ☐ Desired Assertiveness
☐ Enthusiastic ☐ Calms down quickly

Negative: ☐ Difficult to calm ☐ Fails to calm down ☐ Unresponsive ☐ Insecure ☐ Shy
☐ Nervous ☐ Restless ☐ Undesired Aggression ☐ Left area _____ times

RESULT:	☐ Passed	☐ Deferred	☐ Failed

Comments: _____

Date: _____ **Evaluators:** _____

Candidate: _____

Included by permission of the EMDCGB and based on the original SKES form

GLOSSARY

Ankörung - breeding test established in Switzerland covering health, conformation to breed standard and character of the dogs.

Dam - another name for the mother or a litter

Fédération Cynologique Internationale (FCI) - The international body responsible for pedigree dogs in the majority of countries around the world. The Kennel Clubs of most countries are members of the FCI. The UK Kennel Club, the American Kennel Club and the Canadian Kennel Club are not members but do have cooperation agreements in place.

Import Register - the initial recognition by the UK Kennel Club when a breed new to the UK is first brought into the country. Progress to full recognition depends on a number of factors including a significant number of the breed and a clear programme for its ongoing development.

Inbreeding Coefficient or Coefficient of Inbreeding (COI)- the calculation of the probability of a specific gene being repeated, calculated from the repeat ancestors over a specific number of generations.

Sire - another name for the father of the litter

v or v d - In the names of Swiss dogs, 'v' is an abbreviation of 'von' meaning 'from' and 'v d' is 'von der' meaning 'from the'.

REFERENCE MATERIAL

Enzyklopädie der Rassehunde, Band 1: Ursprung, Geschichte, Zuchtziele, Eignung und Verwendung Hans Räber

Der Entlebucher Sennenhund - Dr med. vet. B Kobler - Verlag Paul Haupt Bern

Theriogenology 95 (2017) 163e170 - Factors influencing litter size and puppy losses in the Entlebucher Mountain dog - J. Schrack(a), G. Dolf (b), I.M. Reichler (a), C. Schelling (a), - (a) Clinic of Animal Reproductive Medicine, Department for Farm Animals, Vetsuisse-Faculty, University of Zurich, Winterthurerstrasse 260, 8057 Zurich, Switzerland (b) Institute of Genetics, Vetsuisse-Faculty, University of Berne, Bremgartenstrasse 109a, 3012 Berne, Switzerland

SSV-Kurier 4 -2016

Entlebucher Sennenhund - Christel Fechler (Kosmos)

De Entlebucher Sennenhond - Herma Cornelese 2008

The MacDonald Encyclopedia of Dogs 1983

RECORD OF SEASONS

	Date / Days etc.
Shedding coat	
First day of bleeding	
Ready to receive stud dog	
Weeks & Days since start of previous season	
Other notes	

	Date / Days etc.
Shedding coat	
First day of bleeding	
Ready to receive stud dog	
Weeks & Days since start of previous season	
Other notes	

	Date / Days etc.
Shedding coat	
First day of bleeding	
Ready to receive stud dog	
Weeks & Days since start of previous season	
Other notes	

	Date / Days etc.
Shedding coat	
First day of bleeding	
Ready to receive stud dog	
Weeks & Days since start of previous season	
Other notes	

	Date / Days etc.
Shedding coat	
First day of bleeding	
Ready to receive stud dog	
Weeks & Days since start of previous season	
Other notes	

PROGESTERONE TEST RECORD

Date	Day of Season	Result

Date	Day of Season	Result

Date	Day of Season	Result

LITTERS

Stud Dog: Dam:

Date of Birth:

Name	M/F	Time of birth	Weight	Breeched Y/N	Dew claws	Other notes

Stud Dog: Dam:

Date of Birth:

Name	M/F	Time of birth	Weight	Breeched Y/N	Dew claws	Other notes

NOTES

ROSEMARY J. KIND

Rosemary J. Kind writes because she has to. You could take almost anything away from her except her pen and paper. Failing to stop after the book that everyone has in them, she has gone on to publish books in both non-fiction and fiction, the latter including novels, humour, short stories and poetry. She also regularly produces magazine articles in a number of areas and writes regularly for the dog press.

For twenty years she followed a traditional business career, before seeing the error of her ways and leaving it all behind to pursue her writing full-time.

She spends her life discussing her plots with the characters in her head and her faithful dogs, who always put the opposing arguments when there are choices to be made.

Always willing to take on challenges that sensible people regard as impossible, her hobby is developing the Entlebucher Mountain Dog in the UK. She is Chairman of the EMDCGB – the UK breed club.

She started writing Alfie's Diary as an Internet blog the day Alfie arrived to live with her, intending to continue for a year or two. Twelve years later it goes from strength to strength and has recently been listed as the number three pet blog in the UK.

For more details about the author please visit her website at www.rjkind.co.uk

For more details about her dogs then you're better visiting www.alfiedog.me.uk

(With the author in the picture are Wilma vom Rickental, Cara Isabella vom Kornried and Zebedee Salvatore vom Kornried)

OTHER BOOKS BY ROSEMARY J. KIND

Alfie's Diary

Alfie's Woods

From Story Idea to Reader

Lovers Take up Less Space

New York Orphan

Pet Dogs Democratic Party Manifesto

Poems for Life

The Appearance of Truth

The Lifetracer

Printed in Great Britain
by Amazon

23426764R00117